HAWAII TRAVEL GUIDE 2025

Top Attractions on Maui's Beaches, Oahu's Thrilling Adventures, Big Island's Volcanoes, and Kauai's Secret Treasures

NANCY T. WHITE

MAP OF HAWAII

Na Pali Coast, Hanalei, Mt. Waialeale, Kapaa, Kauai, Waimea Canyon, Poipu Beach

Banzai Pipeline, Waimea Bay, Oahu, Laie, Kahaluu, Makaha, Kualapuu, Wailau Valley, Pearl Harbor, Maunaloa, Honolulu, Diamond Head, Kaunakakai, Molokai, Kaanapali, Lahaina, Maui, Lanai, Kahului, Hana, Lanai City, Wailea, Haleakala, Kahoolawe

HAWAII

40 mi
40 km

N

Pacific Ocean

Kohala Mts., Honokaa, Kohala Coast, Mauna Kea, Hilo, Kailua-Kona, Mauna Loa, Kilauea, Captain Cook, Kona Coast

Kilauea, Kauai, Lihue, Waimea, Niihau, Hawaiian Islands, Waimea, Oahu, Wahiawa, Kaneohe, Pearl City, Ewa Beach, Honolulu, Pearl Harbor, Kanai Channel, Kaiwi Channel, Molokai, Maui, Kaunakakai, Lahaina, Wailuku, Kailua, Lanai, Hana, Lanai City, Kihei, Haleakala 10,023ft (3055m), Kahoolawe, Alenuihaha Channel, Upolu Point, Hawi, Honokaa, Waimea, Keahole Point, Honokohau, Mauna Kea 13,796ft (4205m), Hilo, Keaau, Mauna Loa 13,678ft (4169m), Captain Cook, Hawaii, Volcano, Kilauea 13,379ft (4078m), Kauna Point, Naalehu, Ka Lae

PACIFIC OCEAN

CONTENT

Aloha Spirit: Welcome to Hawaii

Welcome Adventurer **!!!**

The moment I arrived in Hawaii, I felt something different in the air. The warm ocean breeze touched my skin, carrying the scent of tropical flowers and saltwater. As I walked through the airport, I saw smiling locals greeting visitors with open hearts, their kindness feeling as natural as the waves that crashed along the shore. I had heard of the *Aloha Spirit* before, but now I was experiencing it firsthand. It wasn't just a word people used—it was a way of life. A feeling of warmth, kindness, and connection, not only to people but to the land itself.

Hawaii is more than just a tropical paradise—it's a place that changes you. The moment you step onto its shores, you feel a shift, as if the everyday stress of life suddenly fades away. Here, the sun seems to shine brighter, the ocean glows a deeper shade of blue, and time slows down, allowing you to truly take in the beauty around you. Whether you're standing at the edge of a volcano, feeling the heat of the Earth beneath your feet, or watching a fiery sunset paint the sky with colors you've never seen before, Hawaii has a way of making every moment feel special.

But Hawaii is not just about beautiful landscapes—it has a rich history and culture that make it even more fascinating. The islands were home to Polynesian voyagers long before they became a tourist destination. Ancient Hawaiians lived in harmony with nature, believing the land, ocean, and sky were all connected. Today, their traditions live on through music, dance, and storytelling, reminding visitors that Hawaii is not just a place to see but a culture to experience.

In this chapter, we'll explore everything you need to know before your trip—what makes each island unique, the best times to visit, and essential tips to help you travel respectfully and make the most of your time. You'll also learn how to embrace the *Aloha Spirit* in your own journey, ensuring that your experience is more than just a vacation—it's a true adventure that stays with you long after you leave.

Hawaii is calling. Are you ready to answer? *Aloha!*

Introduction to Hawaii

Picture a place where emerald-green mountains rise dramatically from the ocean, waterfalls tumble down cliffs into hidden pools, and the air is filled with the sweet scent of tropical flowers. That place is **Hawaii**—a paradise like no other, brimming with stunning landscapes, vibrant culture, and an energy that calms the soul.

Hawaii is more than just a destination—it's an experience. It's the rhythm of the ocean waves, the warmth of the golden sun on your skin, and the soothing sound of a ukulele in the distance. Whether you're drawn to its world-renowned beaches, powerful volcanoes, or lush rainforests, Hawaii offers an adventure that is both exhilarating and deeply peaceful.

Located in the heart of the Pacific Ocean, Hawaii is the only U.S. state composed entirely of islands. Each island has its own distinct character, from the lively spirit of **Oahu** to the tranquil beauty of **Kauai**. The **Big Island** features some of the most dramatic landscapes on Earth, with active lava flows and snow-capped peaks, while **Maui** is famous for its pristine beaches and the legendary **Road to Hana**. Smaller islands like **Lanai** and **Molokai** offer untouched beauty, providing visitors a glimpse into a quieter, more traditional way of life.

Beyond its breathtaking scenery, Hawaii is steeped in tradition and history. The islands were first settled by Polynesian voyagers over a thousand years ago, bringing with them a rich culture of storytelling, dance, and reverence for nature. Today, Hawaii continues to honor these traditions through **hula performances**, Hawaiian chants, and the continued use of the **Hawaiian language**. Visitors will quickly discover that Hawaii is not just a place to explore—it's a place to connect, learn, and be inspired.

In this chapter, we'll dive deeper into what makes Hawaii so extraordinary. You'll uncover its fascinating history, learn the best times to visit, and explore what makes each island unique. Whether it's your first visit or your tenth, Hawaii has a way of making every trip feel like a fresh adventure.

So take a deep breath, let the **Aloha Spirit** fill your heart, and get ready to experience the magic of Hawaii.

Why Visit Hawaii in 2025?

Hawaii has always been a dream destination, but **2025** is shaping up to be one of the best years to visit. With new travel experiences, thrilling cultural events, and a renewed emphasis on sustainable tourism, there's never been a better time to explore the Aloha State. Whether it's your first time or you're returning for another adventure, Hawaii in 2025 offers exciting opportunities to immerse yourself in its stunning beauty, rich cultural heritage, and exceptional hospitality.

Fewer Crowds, More Authentic Experiences

Following the tourism boom of recent years, Hawaii is now prioritizing responsible tourism, encouraging travelers to explore with greater cultural awareness and a deep respect for nature. In 2025, new travel policies are being introduced to safeguard fragile ecosystems while still offering visitors the chance to experience the island's stunning beaches, lush rainforests, and vibrant coral reefs. This means you'll have more opportunities to enjoy Hawaii's natural beauty without the crowds, ensuring a more peaceful and sustainable experience.

Incredible Weather & Year-Round Adventure

With its warm tropical climate, Hawaii is an ideal destination year-round. Whether you're looking to catch winter waves on **Oahu's North Shore**, hike through **Maui's bamboo forests** in the spring, or unwind on **Kauai's golden beaches** in the summer, 2025 offers unforgettable outdoor adventures. Seasonal events like whale watching, vibrant cultural festivals, and night snorkeling with manta rays ensure that every month is a perfect time to visit.

Revitalized Hawaiian Culture & Festivals

Hawaii is embracing its roots now more than ever, with 2025 marking an important year for preserving and celebrating its indigenous traditions. Visitors can experience immersive cultural events like the **Merrie Monarch Festival** (a world-famous hula competition), **Prince Kuhio Day celebrations**, and **Hawaii Food & Wine Festival**, where traditional flavors meet modern culinary artistry. Learning about Hawaii's history through storytelling, music, and dance has never been more enriching.

Stunning Natural Wonders & Adventure Awaits

Hawaii is home to some of the most diverse landscapes on Earth, and 2025 offers new ways to explore them. Hike to newly accessible lava flows on the Big Island, snorkel in recently restored marine conservation areas, or witness breathtaking sunrises from the summit of Haleakalā. Whether you're chasing waterfalls, walking through lava tubes, or sailing along the Nā Pali Coast, Hawaii's outdoor adventures remain unmatched.

Sustainable & Eco-Friendly Travel Options

Hawaii is leading the way in eco-tourism, and 2025 brings even more opportunities for travelers to experience the islands responsibly. Many resorts are now focused on sustainability, using solar energy and water conservation efforts, while new eco-tours offer ethical encounters with wildlife and support local conservation projects. Travelers can also take part in beach cleanups, tree-planting programs, and Hawaiian cultural preservation initiatives, making a positive impact while enjoying their trip.

A Perfect Escape for Every Traveler

Whether you're a honeymooner seeking a romantic getaway, a family looking for kid-friendly adventures, or a solo traveler in search of relaxation and self-discovery, Hawaii in 2025 offers something for everyone. From luxury beach resorts and boutique eco-lodges to charming local homestays, there's an accommodation style to match your travel goals.

Hawaii is more than just a vacation—it's an experience that stays with you. In 2025, this island paradise is offering visitors a chance to explore its wonders in a more meaningful way, with deeper cultural appreciation and unforgettable moments. So pack your bags, embrace the *Aloha Spirit*, and get ready for the adventure of a lifetime!

Essential Travel Tips & Best Times to Visit

Hawaii is one of the most beautiful and welcoming destinations in the world, but to truly make the most of your trip, it's important to plan wisely. From choosing the right time to visit to understanding local customs and travel essentials, a little preparation can turn a good vacation into an unforgettable experience. In this chapter, you'll find the best travel tips to help you explore Hawaii with ease, respect, and a sense of adventure.

Best Times to Visit Hawaii

Hawaii is a year-round paradise, but depending on your travel goals, some months may be better suited for your trip.

Peak Season (December – April, June – August)

- Ideal for escaping winter and enjoying perfect beach weather.
- Great for whale watching (January – March).
- More festivals and events, but also larger crowds and higher prices.

Shoulder Season (April – June, September – mid-December)

- Best time for fewer crowds and lower hotel rates.
- Ideal for hiking, snorkeling, and enjoying uncrowded beaches.
- Pleasant weather with minimal rainfall.

Hurricane Season (June – November)

- Rare but possible storms; August and September are the most active months.
- Still a great time to visit, with lower costs and warm ocean waters for snorkeling and surfing.

For the perfect balance of good weather, affordability, and fewer tourists, **April, May, September, and October** are often considered the best months to visit Hawaii.

Essential Travel Tips for Hawaii

Hawaii has a warm climate year-round, but different islands and elevations can bring unexpected weather changes. So wear -
✔ Lightweight, breathable clothing for warm beach days.
✔ A light jacket or sweater for cooler nights and mountain areas.
✔ Comfortable hiking shoes for exploring trails and lava fields.

✔ Reef-safe sunscreen to protect the ocean and marine life.
✔ A reusable water bottle to stay hydrated and reduce plastic waste.

Respect the Land & Hawaiian Culture

Hawaii's natural beauty is sacred to the local culture, and protecting it is a top priority.
✔ Never take lava rocks or sand—it's considered bad luck (and illegal in some places).
✔ Respect wildlife by keeping a safe distance from sea turtles, monk seals, and other animals.
✔ Learn a few Hawaiian phrases like **"Mahalo"** (thank you) and **"Aloha"** (hello/goodbye).
✔ Honor sacred sites by following posted signs and not disturbing the area.

Book in Advance, Especially for Popular Attractions

Hawaii's top attractions can sell out quickly, especially during peak season.
✔ Reserve Haleakalā sunrise permits **months in advance**.
✔ Book **Pearl Harbor and snorkeling tours** ahead of time.
✔ Secure inter-island flights early to get the best deals.

Choose the Right Transportation

Getting around Hawaii varies depending on the island you're visiting.
✔ **Oahu:** Public transportation and rideshares work well; rental cars are optional.
✔ **Maui, Big Island, and Kauai:** Renting a car is highly recommended.
✔ **Inter-Island Travel:** Flights are the most reliable way to travel between islands.

Be Mindful of Island Time

Hawaii operates at a slower pace, and rushing through your itinerary can take away from the experience.
✔ Allow for extra time when driving—scenic roads like the Road to Hana are meant to be enjoyed.
✔ Be patient in restaurants and shops—Hawaiians value a laid-back lifestyle.

Support Local Businesses

Hawaii's economy relies on tourism, and supporting local businesses makes a real impact.
✔ Eat at family-run restaurants and food trucks serving authentic Hawaiian cuisine.
✔ Buy handmade souvenirs from local artisans instead of mass-produced items.
✔ Stay in locally owned accommodations when possible.

Practice Eco-Friendly & Sustainable Travel

Hawaii is home to fragile ecosystems that need protection.
- ✔ Use reef-safe sunscreen to prevent coral reef damage.
- ✔ Avoid stepping on coral while snorkeling or diving.
- ✔ Take reusable shopping bags—Hawaii has banned plastic bags.
- ✔ Leave no trace—always clean up after yourself and dispose of waste properly.

By following these essential travel tips and choosing the best time to visit, you'll ensure your Hawaiian adventure is smooth, enjoyable, and respectful of the land and its people. Hawaii isn't just a place to visit—it's an experience to cherish. Embrace the *Aloha Spirit*, plan wisely, and get ready to create unforgettable memories!

Exploring the Hawaiian Islands

The first time I visited Hawaii, I made a common mistake—I thought of it as a single destination. I imagined stepping off the plane, onto a picture-perfect beach, and checking "Hawaii" off my bucket list. But as I quickly learned, Hawaii isn't just one island—it's a collection of stunningly diverse islands, each with its own unique personality, landscapes, and experiences.

I began my journey on **Oahu**, captivated by the vibrant energy of **Waikiki**, the rich history of **Pearl Harbor**, and the world-famous waves of the **North Shore**. But when I arrived on **Kauai**, I felt like I had entered an entirely different world—lush jungles, dramatic cliffs, and hidden waterfalls made it feel like a dream. Then came the **Big Island**, where I stood on the edge of an active volcano, watching molten lava glow against the night sky. **Maui** greeted me with the most stunning sunrise I had ever seen, high above the clouds at **Haleakalā**. And finally, the lesser-known islands of **Molokai** and **Lanai**, where time seemed to slow down and the true spirit of old Hawaii came alive.

What I discovered was simple—Hawaii isn't just one place. It's many places, many stories, and countless adventures waiting to be explored. Each island offers something uniquely special.

In this chapter, we'll take a closer look at the Hawaiian Islands—what makes each one stand out, which islands are best suited for different types of travelers, and how to choose the perfect island (or islands!) for your visit. Whether you're chasing waterfalls, hiking volcanoes, snorkeling in crystal-clear waters, or simply soaking in the **Aloha Spirit**, Hawaii has an island calling your name.

Are you ready to explore? Let's dive in.

Overview of the Main Islands

Hawaii isn't just one destination—it's a collection of islands, each with its own distinct personality, landscapes, and experiences. Whether you're seeking the vibrancy of city life, the solitude of remote natural beauty, or a deep dive into Hawaiian culture, there's an island that feels like it was made just for you.

Here, we'll take a glimpse into Hawaii's six main islands—**Oahu**, **Maui**, **Big Island (Hawai'i)**, **Kauai**, **Molokai**, and **Lanai**—exploring what makes each of them unique and offering a taste of what to expect during your adventure.

Throughout this book, I'll dive deeper into each island in their own chapters, but for now, consider this an overview of what each island has to offer. Each one promises something different, and knowing what you're looking for will help you choose the perfect destination for your Hawaiian getaway.

Oahu: The Heartbeat of Hawaii

If you want a mix of **vibrant city life, stunning beaches, and deep history**, Oahu is the place to be. Home to the state capital, **Honolulu**, Oahu is where **modern luxury meets traditional Hawaiian culture**, offering everything from world-class surfing to historical landmarks and fine dining.

Top Highlights of Oahu

✔ **Waikiki Beach** – Hawaii's most famous beach, with golden sands, turquoise waters, and nonstop energy. Perfect for first-time surfers.
   ✔ **Pearl Harbor & USS Arizona Memorial** – A deeply moving experience where history comes to life.
   ✔ **Diamond Head Crater** – An iconic volcanic cone offering panoramic views of Honolulu after a short hike.
   ✔ **North Shore** – Legendary surf breaks like Banzai Pipeline and Sunset Beach, along with laid-back local vibes.
   ✔ **Hanauma Bay** – One of the best snorkeling spots in Hawaii, filled with vibrant marine life.
   ✔ **Byodo-In Temple** – A hidden gem, this peaceful Buddhist temple sits at the foot of lush mountains.

Best for Travelers Who Want:

✔ A mix of city and beach life
✔ Rich history and cultural experiences
✔ Easy access to shopping, dining, and nightlife
✔ Family-friendly attractions

Maui: The Island of Romance & Adventure

Maui is often called *The Valley Isle*, and it's the perfect balance between **luxurious relaxation and thrilling outdoor adventure**. Known for **some of the best beaches in the world, epic road trips, and breathtaking sunrises**, Maui is a dream for honeymooners, families, and adventure seekers alike.

Top Highlights of Maui

✔ **Haleakalā National Park** – Witness a sunrise above the clouds at over 10,000 feet, or stargaze in one of the world's best dark-sky locations.
✔ **The Road to Hana** – A legendary scenic drive with waterfalls, bamboo forests, and black sand beaches.
✔ **Molokini Crater** – A partially submerged volcanic crater offering unbeatable snorkeling and diving.
✔ **Lahaina & Kaanapali Beach** – Beautiful oceanfront resorts, whale-watching tours, and historic sites.
✔ **Iao Valley** – A lush rainforest with sacred Hawaiian history and stunning green peaks.

Best for Travelers Who Want:

✔ Romantic getaways and luxury resorts
✔ Epic road trips and outdoor adventures
✔ Stunning beaches with great snorkeling and whale-watching opportunities
✔ A balance of relaxation and exploration

Big Island (Hawai'i): The Land of Fire and Ice

The **Big Island** (officially named *Hawai'i*) is the **largest and most diverse island**, featuring **volcanoes, rainforests, black sand beaches, and even snow-capped mountains**. If you want to feel like you're traveling through **multiple planets in one trip**, this is your island.

Top Highlights of Big Island

✔ **Hawai'i Volcanoes National Park** – Home to Kīlauea, one of the most active volcanoes in the world, and Mauna Loa, the largest volcano on Earth.
✔ **Punalu'u Black Sand Beach** – A rare and stunning black sand beach, often visited by sea

turtles.

✔ **Mauna Kea Summit** – Stargazing from the highest peak in Hawaii, often dusted with snow.

✔ **Akaka & Rainbow Falls** – Lush waterfalls hidden in the tropical rainforest.

✔ **Kona Coffee Farms** – Visit world-famous coffee plantations and taste freshly brewed Hawaiian coffee.

✔ **Kealakekua Bay** – A historic bay with incredible snorkeling and the site where Captain Cook first landed in Hawaii.

Best for Travelers Who Want:

✔ A mix of adventure and raw nature
✔ Volcano exploration and unique landscapes
✔ Amazing hiking, waterfalls, and remote beaches
✔ Stargazing and coffee farm experiences

Kauai: The Garden Isle

Kauai is **Hawaii's most rugged and untouched island**, with **lush jungles, towering sea cliffs, and hidden waterfalls**. If you want to **disconnect from the modern world and immerse yourself in nature**, Kauai is where you should go.

Top Highlights of Kauai

✔ **Nā Pali Coast** – One of the most jaw-dropping coastlines in the world, best explored by boat, helicopter, or the famous Kalalau Trail.

✔ **Waimea Canyon** – Known as the *Grand Canyon of the Pacific*, this dramatic landscape is filled with colorful cliffs and waterfalls.

✔ **Hanalei Bay** – A picturesque bay surrounded by lush mountains, offering the perfect mix of beach relaxation and adventure.

✔ **Wailua Falls & Secret Falls** – Stunning waterfalls accessible by kayak or short hikes.

✔ **Poipu Beach** – One of the best beaches for spotting Hawaiian monk seals.

Best for Travelers Who Want:

✔ Untouched nature and rugged beauty
✔ Epic hiking and off-the-grid adventures
✔ Quiet, laid-back beaches and charming small towns
✔ Dramatic cliffs, waterfalls, and jungle landscapes

Molokai: The Most Authentic Hawaiian Island

Molokai is **Hawaii's least developed and most traditional island**—there are **no big resorts, no traffic lights, and no large crowds**. It's **Hawaii as it once was**, offering a glimpse into **a slower, more authentic Hawaiian lifestyle**.

Top Highlights of Molokai

✔ **Kalaupapa National Historical Park** – A secluded former leprosy colony with a powerful history and stunning sea cliffs.
✔ **Papohaku Beach** – One of Hawaii's longest and emptiest white sand beaches.
✔ **Halawa Valley** – A hidden valley with ancient Polynesian temples and a stunning waterfall hike.
✔ **Molokai Sea Cliffs** – Some of the **tallest sea cliffs in the world**, best viewed from the ocean or a small plane.

Best for Travelers Who Want:

✔ A slow, traditional, and culturally rich experience
✔ Zero crowds and an off-the-beaten-path adventure
✔ Beautiful, uncrowded beaches and hiking trails
✔ An opportunity to connect with local Hawaiian communities

Lanai: The Private Island Escape

Lanai is **Hawaii's smallest inhabited island**, known for its **secluded luxury resorts, rugged landscapes, and otherworldly rock formations**. With only **3,000 residents and limited tourist development**, Lanai offers an **exclusive and tranquil escape**.

Top Highlights of Lanai

✔ **Hulopo'e Bay** – A postcard-perfect beach with crystal-clear water and excellent snorkeling.
✔ **Keahiakawelo (Garden of the Gods)** – A surreal, Mars-like rock landscape unique to Lanai.
✔ **Shipwreck Beach** – A long, empty beach with the remains of a WWII-era shipwreck.
✔ **Polihua Beach** – One of Hawaii's most secluded, untouched beaches.

Best for Travelers Who Want:

✔ Seclusion and privacy
✔ Unique landscapes with a rugged, remote feel
✔ A quiet, luxurious retreat

Which Hawaiian Island is Right for You?

- **For first-time visitors & city lovers: Oahu**
- **For luxury, romance & adventure: Maui**
- **For outdoor lovers & volcano chasers: Big Island**
- **For remote jungle & hiking enthusiasts: Kauai**
- **For a deep cultural experience: Molokai**
- **For seclusion & exclusivity: Lanai**

No matter which island you choose, Hawaii will **capture your heart** and leave you longing to return. **Why pick just one?** The magic of Hawaii is best experienced by exploring multiple islands, each offering a completely different side of paradise.

Choosing the Best Island for Your Trip

Hawaii is not a single destination—it's a collection of islands, each with its own unique charm, landscapes, and culture. Choosing the right island for your trip is crucial to ensuring you get the experience you're looking for. Whether you're dreaming of white sandy beaches, towering volcanoes, lush rainforests, or vibrant city life, there's an island that perfectly suits your travel style.

In this chapter, we'll break down which Hawaiian island is best based on **your travel preferences, budget, and must-have experiences**. You'll also discover why many visitors choose to explore more than one island during their trip.

Oahu – Best for First-Time Visitors & City Lovers

If you're visiting Hawaii for the first time and want a little bit of everything, **Oahu** is the perfect place to start. Known as *The Gathering Place*, Oahu offers a **blend of history, culture, nightlife, and stunning beaches**. Home to **Honolulu**, the state capital, and **Waikiki Beach**, the island has a bustling energy while still offering plenty of nature and adventure.

Oahu is the most developed and accessible island, with **the largest airport (Daniel K. Inouye International Airport - HNL)** and direct flights from major international and U.S.

cities. This makes it an ideal choice for travelers who want an easy, well-rounded Hawaiian experience. You can **explore the history of Pearl Harbor in the morning, surf on the North Shore in the afternoon, and dine at a world-class restaurant by evening.**

Despite its urban appeal, Oahu is also home to incredible natural wonders. You can **hike up Diamond Head Crater** for a breathtaking view of Honolulu, snorkel at **Hanauma Bay**, or escape the crowds by driving to **Lanikai Beach**, known for its soft white sand and crystal-clear waters. Oahu's diverse landscape ensures that whether you're seeking adventure, relaxation, or cultural immersion, you'll find it here.

- *Perfect for*: First-time visitors, families, history lovers, and those who want nightlife and convenience.
- *Must-Do Experiences*: Pearl Harbor, Waikiki Beach, Diamond Head hike, North Shore surfing, Hanauma Bay snorkeling.

Maui – Best for Romance, Beaches & Scenic Drives

Maui is the ultimate **romantic getaway** and a paradise for those who love **luxury, relaxation, and outdoor adventure**. Known as *The Valley Isle*, Maui is famous for its **gorgeous beaches, breathtaking sunrises, and the iconic Road to Hana**—one of the most scenic drives in the world.

If you're looking for **high-end resorts and stunning beaches**, Maui is the best choice. The **Wailea and Kaanapali** areas are home to world-class resorts, offering **spa treatments, oceanfront dining, and some of the most beautiful sunset views in Hawaii**.

For adventure seekers, Maui is packed with once-in-a-lifetime experiences. Watching the **sunrise from the summit of Haleakalā**, Maui's 10,000-foot dormant volcano, is a surreal experience. Driving the **Road to Hana** takes you through lush rainforests, past cascading waterfalls, and to hidden black and red sand beaches. Snorkeling and diving at **Molokini Crater**, a crescent-shaped islet, offers some of the best underwater views in Hawaii.

Maui's mix of adventure and relaxation makes it the **perfect island for honeymooners, couples, and those looking for both excitement and serenity.**

- *Perfect for*: Honeymooners, couples, beach lovers, and luxury travelers.
- *Must-Do Experiences*: Road to Hana, Haleakalā sunrise, whale watching (winter months), Molokini snorkeling.

Big Island – Best for Volcanoes & Outdoor Adventures

If you're fascinated by **raw, untouched nature and dramatic landscapes**, the Big Island (officially named *Hawai'i*) is the place to go. As **the youngest and largest island in the Hawaiian chain**, it offers **everything from snow-capped mountains to active lava flows, black sand beaches, and lush rainforests**—making it feel like you're visiting multiple worlds in one trip.

The biggest draw of the Big Island is **Hawai'i Volcanoes National Park**, home to **Kīlauea**, one of the world's most active volcanoes, and **Mauna Loa**, the largest volcano on Earth. Walking through lava tubes, witnessing glowing lava flows, and exploring ancient craters offer an unforgettable experience for any adventure traveler.

Beyond its volcanoes, the Big Island is **one of the best places in the world for stargazing**. At nearly 14,000 feet, **Mauna Kea's summit** offers an unparalleled view of the cosmos, making it a must-visit for astronomy lovers.

The Big Island also has **beautiful beaches, lush valleys, and world-renowned coffee farms in Kona**. If you want to experience the power of nature up close and don't mind driving long distances, this is the island for you.

- *Perfect for*: Adventure seekers, nature lovers, hikers, and those who want unique landscapes.
- *Must-Do Experiences*: Hawai'i Volcanoes National Park, Mauna Kea Observatory, Punalu'u Black Sand Beach, Kona coffee tasting.

Kauai – Best for Secluded Nature & Hiking

Kauai, also known as *The Garden Isle*, is the **greenest and most rugged** of the Hawaiian islands. If you're looking for **dramatic cliffs, lush jungles, and stunning waterfalls**, Kauai is the island for you. Unlike the other islands, Kauai has very little development, making it **the perfect place to disconnect from the modern world** and immerse yourself in nature.

One of the biggest draws of Kauai is the **Nā Pali Coast**, one of the most spectacular coastlines in the world. With **towering sea cliffs, hidden beaches, and lush valleys**, it's a must-see, whether you hike the **Kalalau Trail**, take a **helicopter tour**, or explore it by boat.

Another highlight is **Waimea Canyon**, often called *The Grand Canyon of the Pacific*. This massive red-rock canyon, with its breathtaking waterfalls and hiking trails, offers some of the best views in Hawaii.

For those who love remote, off-the-beaten-path experiences, Kauai delivers with **secluded beaches, lush rainforests, and small, charming towns**.

- *Perfect for*: Hikers, nature lovers, photographers, and those seeking peace and quiet.
- *Must-Do Experiences*: Nā Pali Coast, Waimea Canyon, Hanalei Bay, Secret Falls kayaking.

Molokai & Lanai – Best for Seclusion & Cultural Experiences

For travelers who want to **avoid crowds and experience the most traditional side of Hawaii, Molokai and Lanai** are perfect choices. These islands offer **few tourists, untouched landscapes, and a strong connection to native Hawaiian culture**.

- **Molokai** is often called **the most Hawaiian island**, as it remains largely untouched by tourism. Here, you'll find **remote beaches, the world's tallest sea cliffs, and sacred historical sites**.
- **Lanai** is a mix of **luxury and adventure**, offering **secluded beaches, rugged landscapes, and one of the most exclusive resorts in Hawaii (Four Seasons Lanai)**.

These islands are best for those looking for a **quiet, authentic, and crowd-free escape**.

- *Perfect for*: Off-the-grid travelers, history buffs, and those who want an authentic Hawaiian experience.
- *Must-Do Experiences*: Kalaupapa National Park (Molokai), Shipwreck Beach (Lanai), Hulopo'e Bay snorkeling.

Should You Visit More Than One Island?

If you can't decide, **why not visit more than one island?** Many travelers choose to **split their trip between two or more islands**, experiencing the best of each. Oahu and Maui make a great combination, while Big Island and Kauai offer an unforgettable contrast of landscapes.

No matter which island you choose, Hawaii promises an experience like no other—one filled with adventure, relaxation, and the warm embrace of the *Aloha Spirit*.

Inter-Island Travel & Transportation

Hawaii may be a chain of islands, but traveling between them isn't as simple as crossing a bridge or driving a few miles. With vast stretches of open ocean separating each island, travelers must rely on flights, ferries, cruises, or private charters to move from one destination to the next. Unlike many other tropical spots, Hawaii has limited inter-island transport options, so careful planning is essential to avoid wasting precious vacation time.

Many visitors arrive in Hawaii with the idea of exploring multiple islands in a single trip, but the reality is that island-hopping requires time, money, and patience. **Flights** are the most efficient way to travel between islands, though there are also **ferry services** connecting select islands and **inter-island cruises** that let you experience multiple destinations without the hassle of separate bookings. Knowing the best ways to get between islands—and how to navigate once you arrive—will help ensure you make the most of your time in paradise.

Flying Between Islands: The Fastest and Most Reliable Option

For most travelers, **inter-island flights** are the quickest, most convenient, and practical way to get between the Hawaiian islands. These flights are short, typically lasting between **20 to 50 minutes**, and with numerous airlines offering frequent daily departures, flying is often the best option.

Hawaiian Airlines is the largest and most reliable airline for inter-island travel, operating numerous daily routes between **Oahu, Maui, Big Island**, and **Kauai. Southwest Airlines** also provides budget-friendly inter-island flights, though its routes are more limited. For travelers heading to smaller islands like **Molokai** or **Lanai**, airlines like **Mokulele Airlines** offer smaller commuter flights, often using propeller-driven aircraft that provide stunning aerial views of the ocean and islands below.

While inter-island flights are fast, it's important to book early, especially during peak travel seasons. Unlike mainland U.S. flights, inter-island flights can sell out quickly, and prices often increase as departure dates approach. If you plan to visit multiple islands, it's best to book all your flights at once rather than purchasing them separately during your trip.

Inter-Island Ferries: A Scenic But Limited Option

Unlike many other island destinations, **Hawaii** has very few ferry services between its islands. While ferries once operated between **Maui** and **Molokai**, that service was discontinued in 2016, leaving just one active ferry route in Hawaii today: the **Maui to Lanai ferry**.

The **Expeditions Lanai Ferry** is the only commercial ferry service in Hawaii, operating between **Lahaina Harbor** on **Maui** and **Manele Harbor** on **Lanai**. The journey takes about **45 minutes** and offers stunning ocean views along the way. Many visitors use this ferry for a day trip from Maui to Lanai, as Lanai is a smaller island that can easily be explored in a single day. However, beyond this one route, ferries are not a viable option for inter-island travel, and visitors will need to rely on **flights** for longer distances.

For those who choose the ferry, it's important to check the ocean conditions beforehand, as Hawaii's waters can be choppy, especially in the afternoons when the trade winds pick up. If you're prone to motion sickness, it's a good idea to take medication or bring anti-nausea remedies to ensure a smooth ride.

Private Charters & Helicopter Transfers: A Luxury Option

For those looking for a **private, exclusive, and fast way to island-hop**, **private charters and helicopter transfers** offer a high-end alternative to commercial flights. While these services are significantly **more expensive**, they provide **personalized travel experiences, no airport hassles, and breathtaking aerial views** of Hawaii's islands and ocean.

Private plane charters allow travelers to fly directly between **smaller, less accessible airports**, avoiding busy commercial hubs and long security lines. Helicopter transfers, while even more expensive, provide **once-in-a-lifetime views** of volcanic craters, rainforests, and dramatic coastlines that can't be seen from a commercial airplane.

This type of inter-island travel is ideal for **high-end travelers, honeymooners, and those looking for VIP experiences**, but it comes at a cost—**private charters can start at $1,500 per flight**, while helicopter transfers can cost **anywhere from $500 to $2,000 per person**, depending on the distance and provider.

Inter-Island Cruises: A Hassle-Free Way to See Multiple Islands

For travelers who **want to visit multiple islands without dealing with separate flights or hotel bookings**, a **Hawaiian cruise** is one of the most convenient ways to experience the best of each island. Unlike Caribbean or Mediterranean cruises, **Hawaiian cruises focus on maximizing island time** rather than spending long days at sea.

The **Pride of America (Norwegian Cruise Line)** is **the only U.S.-based cruise ship that sails round-trip from Honolulu** and stops at **Maui, Big Island (Hilo & Kona), and Kauai** in a **7-day itinerary**. This is a **great option for those who don't want to worry about transportation, accommodation, or planning logistics**, as the ship serves as both a hotel and a mode of transportation between islands.

While cruises offer a stress-free way to see multiple islands, the downside is **limited time on each island**. Unlike flying, where you can explore at your own pace, cruise passengers are restricted to the ship's schedule and may only have **one or two days per island** before moving on. Still, for those who prefer an all-in-one package, cruises provide a **comfortable and efficient way to explore multiple islands** in a single trip.

Getting Around Each Island: Transportation Tips

Once you arrive at your destination, you'll need a way to get around. **Hawaii's islands vary greatly in terms of transportation options**, and while some places have public transit, others **require a rental car or guided tours** to fully explore.

Rental Cars: The Best Way to Explore

For most travelers, **renting a car is the best way to explore Hawaii's islands**, especially on **Maui, the Big Island, and Kauai**, where attractions are spread out and public transport is limited. **Oahu, while more urbanized, also benefits from having a rental car if you plan to explore beyond Honolulu.**

Rental car prices can **range from $50 to $150 per day**, depending on demand. **Booking early is crucial,** as rental cars frequently sell out, especially during peak seasons. If you plan on driving the **Road to Hana (Maui)** or **Mauna Kea (Big Island),** be sure to rent a **4WD vehicle**, as some areas have rugged, unpaved roads.

Public Transport: Only Useful on Oahu

If you're staying in **Honolulu and Waikiki, public transport is a great option. TheBus,** Oahu's public transit system, covers most of the island and is **affordable and reliable.** However, **other islands have very limited bus services** that are **not ideal for tourists.**

Taxis & Rideshares: Convenient But Expensive

Uber and Lyft are available on **Oahu, Maui, and Big Island**, but they can be **unreliable in rural areas** and **expensive** for long distances. **Taxis are also costly,** so most visitors prefer rental cars or guided tours.

Guided Tours: A No-Driving Option

For those who don't want to rent a car, **guided tours are an excellent alternative**. **Road to Hana tours (Maui), Volcano National Park tours (Big Island), and Nā Pali Coast boat tours (Kauai)** are some of the best options for exploring without the stress of driving.

If you want **speed and convenience, flying is the best choice**. If you prefer a **scenic route**, the **Maui to Lanai ferry is worth considering**. For a **stress-free, all-inclusive experience**, a **Hawaiian cruise allows you to visit multiple islands with ease**. Regardless of how you travel, **island-hopping in Hawaii is an unforgettable experience**—just make sure to plan ahead to **make the most of your adventure.**

Ultimate Hawaii Itinerary: 7 to 14 Days of Adventure

The first time I planned a trip to **Hawaii**, I thought I had everything mapped out. I had a list of must-see spots, from famous beaches to hidden waterfalls, and I was determined to check them all off. But as soon as I landed, reality hit me—Hawaii isn't just one destination, it's a collection of islands, each with its own unique rhythm and charm. I found myself rushing from place to place, trying to squeeze in every attraction, only to realize I was missing the true essence of the islands.

That trip taught me an important lesson: **Hawaii** is best experienced slowly and intentionally. Instead of cramming in every possible activity, I should have taken the time to enjoy the breathtaking sunrises, taken spontaneous detours down scenic roads, and fully embraced the laid-back island lifestyle.

If you're planning a trip to Hawaii, having the right itinerary is crucial. Whether you have one week or two, it's important to balance adventure with relaxation, ensuring that you experience the natural wonders, cultural traditions, and unforgettable moments that make Hawaii so special.

In this section, you'll find a **7-day itinerary** for those looking to experience the highlights of one or two islands, as well as a **14-day itinerary** for travelers seeking a deeper, multi-island adventure. No matter which option you choose, this guide will help you make the most of your time without feeling rushed or overwhelmed. Let's dive in and craft the perfect Hawaiian getaway.

One-Week Highlights for First-Time Visitors

Planning a one-week trip to Hawaii can feel overwhelming, especially if it's your first visit. With so many breathtaking landscapes, outdoor adventures, and cultural experiences, it's easy to feel like you need to see it all. But Hawaii isn't meant to be rushed. Instead of trying to visit multiple islands in a short amount of time, the best approach is to **focus on one or two islands** and experience them fully.

For first-time visitors, **Oahu and Maui** offer the perfect mix of **iconic attractions, stunning beaches, and unforgettable adventures**. Oahu is the best choice for those who want a balance of **history, nightlife, and outdoor activities**, while Maui is ideal for those seeking **scenic drives, volcanic landscapes, and pristine beaches**. If you prefer something more rugged and adventurous, **the Big Island or Kauai** can also be excellent choices, but travel time between attractions will be longer.

This **7-day itinerary** is designed to help you **maximize your time without feeling rushed**, covering the best of Oahu and Maui while leaving room for relaxation and spontaneous exploration.

Day 1: Arrival in Oahu & Sunset at Waikiki Beach

Your Hawaiian adventure begins as you land at **Daniel K. Inouye International Airport (HNL)** in Honolulu. After picking up your rental car or taking a shuttle to your accommodation, spend your first afternoon settling in. Waikiki is the heart of Oahu's tourism scene, and while it can be busy, it's the perfect place to start your trip.

- Check into your hotel or resort in **Waikiki** or **nearby Honolulu**.
- Take a stroll along **Waikiki Beach**, where you can soak in the views of **Diamond Head** in the distance.
- If you're up for it, rent a surfboard or take a beginner's surf lesson right on the beach.
- Grab dinner at **Duke's Waikiki**, a famous beachfront restaurant known for fresh seafood and tropical cocktails.
- End your day with a breathtaking **sunset over the Pacific Ocean**.

Day 2: Pearl Harbor & North Shore Adventure

Start your day early with a visit to **Pearl Harbor**, one of Hawaii's most significant historical sites. The **USS Arizona Memorial** offers a moving experience, providing insight into the events of World War II.

- Arrive at **Pearl Harbor Visitor Center** as early as possible (7:00 AM opening).

- Tour the **USS Arizona Memorial** and, if time permits, visit the **Battleship Missouri** and **Pacific Aviation Museum**.
- After Pearl Harbor, drive up to **Oahu's North Shore**—a more laid-back, scenic side of the island.
- Stop at **Laniakea Beach**, also known as "Turtle Beach," to see Hawaiian green sea turtles basking in the sun.
- Grab lunch at a famous **shrimp truck** in **Haleiwa**, such as **Giovanni's Shrimp Truck**.
- Explore the charming surf town of **Haleiwa**, filled with local boutiques and coffee shops.
- If visiting during winter (November to February), watch the world's best surfers ride giant waves at **Banzai Pipeline** and **Sunset Beach**.
- Head back to Waikiki and enjoy a relaxing dinner at **House Without a Key**, offering live Hawaiian music and an oceanfront view.

Day 3: Hike Diamond Head & Snorkel at Hanauma Bay

No trip to Oahu is complete without **hiking Diamond Head**, the island's most famous crater. The early morning is the best time to go, avoiding both crowds and the midday heat.

- Start your morning with the **Diamond Head Summit Hike** (about **1.5–2 hours round trip**). The reward? A **panoramic view of Waikiki and the coastline**.
- After the hike, grab a fresh **acai bowl** or **Hawaiian breakfast** at **Bogart's Café** or **Koko Head Café**.
- Head to **Hanauma Bay**, one of the most famous snorkeling spots in the world. Arrive early, as the number of visitors is limited to **protect the reef**.
- Spend your afternoon snorkeling with **tropical fish and sea turtles** in crystal-clear waters.
- Drive to **Halona Blowhole Lookout** for a scenic stop before heading back to Waikiki.
- Enjoy a sunset dinner at **Michel's at the Colony Surf**, known for oceanfront fine dining.

Day 4: Fly to Maui & Relax on Kaanapali Beach

Your adventure continues as you take a **short 40-minute flight to Maui**. Maui offers a more laid-back, scenic experience compared to Oahu.

- Arrive at **Kahului Airport (OGG)** in Maui and pick up your rental car.
- Drive to **West Maui (Lahaina, Kaanapali, or Kapalua)** and check into your accommodation.
- Spend your afternoon relaxing on **Kaanapali Beach**, one of Maui's most beautiful stretches of sand.

- Enjoy a beachfront dinner at **Leilani's on the Beach** or **Merriman's Kapalua**.
- If you're up for an evening activity, attend a **luau** such as **Old Lahaina Luau**, known for its authenticity.

Day 5: Sunrise at Haleakalā & Road to Hana

Maui's most famous sunrise is waiting for you at **Haleakalā National Park**. You'll need to wake up **very early (around 3 AM)** to drive up the crater and secure a spot for sunrise.

- Watch an **unforgettable sunrise at Haleakalā**, standing above the clouds at **10,000 feet**.
- After the sunrise, start your **Road to Hana adventure**—a full-day scenic drive with waterfalls, black sand beaches, and rainforests.
- Key stops include **Twin Falls, Wailua Overlook, Wai'anapanapa State Park (Black Sand Beach), and Ohe'o Gulch (Seven Sacred Pools)**.
- If time allows, visit **Hana Town** for a meal before heading back to your hotel.

📍 **Alternative Option:** If you don't want to drive the entire Road to Hana, take a guided tour to avoid the stress of navigating the winding roads.

Day 6: Snorkeling at Molokini Crater & Exploring Lahaina

Maui is home to some of **Hawaii's best snorkeling**, and a boat trip to **Molokini Crater** offers a once-in-a-lifetime experience.

- Take a **morning snorkeling tour** to **Molokini Crater**, where you'll swim with tropical fish and possibly spot reef sharks.
- The tour often includes a stop at **Turtle Town**, where you can see Hawaiian green sea turtles up close.
- Spend your afternoon exploring **Lahaina**, a charming town filled with historic sites, art galleries, and local shops.
- Have your final Hawaiian dinner at **Mama's Fish House**, one of Maui's most famous restaurants.

Day 7: Relax & Fly Home

On your final day, take time to **relax and reflect on your trip**. Depending on your flight schedule, you can:

- Spend your morning at **Kapalua Bay**, a quiet and scenic beach perfect for one last swim.
- Visit **Iao Valley**, a lush green valley with stunning mountain peaks.

- Grab a Hawaiian-style breakfast at **Gazebo Restaurant** before heading to the airport.

As you board your flight home, you'll carry with you **memories of island sunsets, volcano sunrises, and the spirit of Aloha**. This **one-week itinerary** ensures that first-time visitors experience the best of Hawaii, balancing **adventure, relaxation, and cultural immersion**.

If one week leaves you wanting more, **a return trip is always a good idea—because no one visits Hawaii just once.**

Two-Week In-Depth Exploration

A single week in Hawaii can feel like a whirlwind—just when you start settling into the island rhythm, it's already time to leave. But if you have **two full weeks**, you can truly experience the depth and diversity of the Hawaiian Islands. This itinerary is designed for those who want to **slow down, explore multiple islands, and dive deeper into Hawaii's landscapes, culture, and adventures** without feeling rushed.

With **14 days**, you'll have time to **visit three or even four islands**, allowing you to experience **the vibrant energy of Oahu, the scenic wonders of Maui, the volcanic landscapes of the Big Island, and the lush rainforests of Kauai.** Each island offers something completely different, from world-famous beaches and waterfalls to stargazing on a dormant volcano and hiking through towering sea cliffs.

This itinerary ensures you **see Hawaii's most iconic sites while also discovering hidden gems**—giving you the best mix of adventure, relaxation, and cultural immersion.

Days 1–3: Oahu – The Heartbeat of Hawaii

Your adventure begins in **Honolulu**, the gateway to Hawaii. Oahu is the most **accessible and action-packed island**, blending modern city life with stunning natural beauty.

Day 1: Arrival & Waikiki Beach

- Land at **Daniel K. Inouye International Airport (HNL)** and check into your hotel in Waikiki or near downtown Honolulu.
- Spend your first afternoon soaking in the views at **Waikiki Beach**, where you can try **surfing, paddleboarding, or simply relax with a mai tai in hand**.
- Enjoy a beachfront dinner at **Duke's Waikiki**, a legendary spot for fresh seafood and live Hawaiian music.

Day 2: Pearl Harbor & North Shore Adventure

- Start your morning early at **Pearl Harbor**, where you'll visit the **USS Arizona Memorial** and learn about the historic events of World War II.
- Drive up to **Oahu's North Shore**, stopping at **Laniakea Beach (Turtle Beach)** to see Hawaiian green sea turtles.
- Explore the charming surf town of **Haleiwa**, filled with food trucks, coffee shops, and local boutiques.
- If visiting during winter (November–February), watch professional surfers ride **Banzai Pipeline's** massive waves.
- Grab dinner at **Haleiwa Joe's**, known for its incredible sunset views.

Day 3: Hike Diamond Head & Snorkel Hanauma Bay

- Begin your morning with a **sunrise hike up Diamond Head**, offering one of the best panoramic views of Waikiki.
- Have breakfast at **Bogart's Café** or **Koko Head Café**, both famous for their local dishes.
- Spend the rest of the day snorkeling at **Hanauma Bay**, a protected marine sanctuary teeming with tropical fish and coral reefs.
- End your Oahu adventure with a scenic drive along the **Windward Coast**, stopping at **Halona Blowhole** and **Lanikai Beach** before heading back to Waikiki.

Days 4–7: Maui – Scenic Drives, Volcanic Sunrises & Pristine Beaches

Maui is known for its **romantic beaches, lush landscapes, and the world-famous Road to Hana**. This island offers a perfect mix of relaxation and adventure.

Day 4: Arrival & Sunset at Kaanapali Beach

- Take a short flight from Oahu to **Maui (Kahului Airport - OGG)**.
- Pick up a rental car and drive to **West Maui**, home to luxury resorts and stunning beaches.
- Spend your afternoon at **Kaanapali Beach**, where you can swim, snorkel, or just relax in the sun.
- Watch the iconic **cliff diving ceremony at Black Rock** before enjoying a sunset dinner at **Leilani's on the Beach**.

Day 5: Sunrise at Haleakalā & Upcountry Maui

- Wake up early (around 3 AM) to drive up to **Haleakalā National Park** and witness an **incredible sunrise above the clouds**.
- After sunrise, explore **Upcountry Maui**, stopping at **Ali'i Kula Lavender Farm** and **MauiWine** for wine tasting.

- Have lunch at **Hali'imaile General Store**, a farm-to-table favorite.
- Spend your evening exploring the historic town of **Lahaina** before enjoying a relaxed beachfront dinner.

Day 6: Road to Hana – The Ultimate Scenic Drive

- Spend a full day driving the **Road to Hana**, one of the most scenic coastal routes in the world.
- Key stops include **Twin Falls, Wailua Overlook, Wai'anapanapa State Park (Black Sand Beach), and Ohe'o Gulch (Seven Sacred Pools).**
- Optional overnight stay in Hana for a more relaxed experience or drive back to West Maui in the evening.

Day 7: Snorkeling at Molokini Crater & Beach Day

- Take a **morning snorkeling tour to Molokini Crater**, where you'll swim with colorful reef fish and possibly spot manta rays.
- Have a relaxing afternoon at **Makena Beach (Big Beach)** or **Kapalua Bay**, both known for their soft sand and clear waters.
- Enjoy a farewell dinner at **Mama's Fish House**, one of Hawaii's most famous restaurants.

Days 8–11: Big Island – Volcanoes & Stargazing

The Big Island is home to **Hawai'i Volcanoes National Park**, dramatic landscapes, black sand beaches, and one of the best stargazing locations in the world.

Day 8: Arrival & Kona Coffee Country

- Fly from Maui to **Kona (KOA)** and pick up your rental car.
- Spend your day touring **Kona's coffee farms**, where you can taste some of the world's best coffee.
- Visit **Punalu'u Black Sand Beach**, a stunning volcanic beach known for its lava-formed sand and sea turtles.
- Check into a resort along the **Kohala Coast** and relax.

Day 9: Hawai'i Volcanoes National Park

- Drive to **Hawai'i Volcanoes National Park**, home to the famous **Kīlauea and Mauna Loa volcanoes**.
- Walk through the **Thurston Lava Tube**, explore the **Jaggar Museum**, and witness **lava flows if active**.

- Return to your hotel or stay overnight in **Volcano Village** for a unique rainforest experience.

Day 10: Mauna Kea Stargazing & Waterfalls

- Visit **Akaka Falls State Park**, home to **one of Hawaii's tallest waterfalls**.
- In the evening, drive up to **Mauna Kea's summit**, one of the world's best locations for stargazing.
- Experience an unforgettable night under the **clearest skies in the Pacific**.

Day 11: Beach Day & Relaxation

- Spend a **relaxing day at Hapuna Beach**, one of the best white-sand beaches in Hawaii.
- Fly to **Kauai in the evening**, settling into your hotel for the next adventure.

Days 12–14: Kauai – The Garden Isle

Kauai is Hawaii's most **lush and dramatic island**, with stunning cliffs, waterfalls, and secluded beaches.

Day 12: Explore the Na Pali Coast

- Take a **Na Pali Coast boat or helicopter tour** for breathtaking views of Hawaii's most rugged coastline.
- Relax at **Hanalei Bay**, a postcard-perfect crescent-shaped beach.

Day 13: Waimea Canyon & Waterfalls

- Drive to **Waimea Canyon**, known as the *Grand Canyon of the Pacific*.
- Visit **Wailua Falls** and hike through **Kokee State Park**.

Day 14: Relax & Fly Home

- Enjoy a final beach day at **Poipu Beach** before heading to the airport.

This two-week itinerary lets you **experience the best of Hawaii without feeling rushed**, blending **adventure, relaxation, and culture**. Whether it's your first visit or a return trip, **Hawaii will always leave you wanting more.**

Best Family-Friendly and Romantic Itineraries

Hawaii is the ultimate destination for both **family vacations** and **romantic getaways**, offering breathtaking landscapes, world-class resorts, and a perfect mix of adventure and relaxation. Whether you're traveling with kids or planning a honeymoon, the islands provide the ideal backdrop for unforgettable experiences. A well-planned itinerary ensures families can enjoy stress-free fun while couples can immerse themselves in romance and tranquility.

For families, **Oahu** and **Maui** are ideal choices. Oahu offers kid-friendly beaches, interactive museums, and cultural attractions, while **Maui** features gentle snorkeling spots, scenic drives, and laid-back resort experiences. This combination allows families to explore Hawaii without feeling rushed, offering activities that entertain children while providing parents with moments of relaxation.

Starting in **Oahu**, families can settle into **Waikiki Beach**, where the waves are gentle, and the sand is perfect for little ones to play. The **Honolulu Zoo** and **Waikiki Aquarium** offer a fun and educational start to the trip, allowing kids to see exotic animals and marine life up close. A visit to **Pearl Harbor** provides a valuable history lesson in an interactive setting, engaging older children, while a drive to Oahu's **North Shore** introduces them to the island's famous sea turtles.

When transitioning to **Maui**, families can unwind at a beachfront resort with kid-friendly pools and activities, giving everyone a chance to recharge. A visit to the **Maui Ocean Center** lets children learn about Hawaiian marine life before heading out to snorkel in **Molokini Crater** or **Turtle Town**, where they can swim alongside vibrant fish and sea turtles. The **Road to Hana**, although long, can be broken up with short hikes, waterfall swims, and stops at fruit stands, making it an adventure kids will never forget.

For couples seeking a **romantic escape**, **Maui** and **Kauai** make the perfect combination. **Maui**, often considered Hawaii's most romantic island, offers sunset beach walks, luxury resorts, and unforgettable sunrises at **Haleakalā National Park**. Starting in **Wailea** or **Kapalua**, couples can settle into a private oceanfront suite, enjoy a spa day with traditional Hawaiian massages, and toast their first evening with a sunset dinner overlooking the Pacific.

Waking up before dawn for a **Haleakalā sunrise** may not sound romantic, but standing above the clouds as the sun paints the sky in shades of orange and pink is one of the most magical moments Hawaii has to offer. Later in the day, the **Road to Hana** provides couples with a scenic adventure, where they can explore hidden waterfalls, secluded beaches, and bamboo forests. The journey itself is as memorable as the destination, with opportunities to stop at roadside stands for fresh banana bread and take in sweeping coastal views.

The second half of the trip takes couples to **Kauai**, Hawaii's most secluded and scenic island. Known as the **Garden Isle**, **Kauai** is home to dramatic cliffs, lush rainforests, and quiet beaches where couples can escape the crowds. A **helicopter tour** over the **Nā Pali Coast** offers one of the most breathtaking views in the world, revealing waterfalls and valleys that are otherwise inaccessible. A private boat tour at sunset, complete with champagne and traditional Hawaiian music, makes for a perfect evening.

For couples who love outdoor adventures, hiking through **Waimea Canyon** provides awe-inspiring views, while **kayaking the Wailua River** to **Secret Falls** adds an element of exploration. Those looking for a slower pace can spend the day at **Hanalei Bay**, watching the waves roll in as they sip cocktails at a beachfront bar. The final evening in Hawaii is best spent at **Poipu Beach**, where couples can watch the sunset together, reflecting on a journey filled with beauty, relaxation, and romance.

Whether traveling as a family or a couple, Hawaii offers something for everyone. Thoughtfully planning an itinerary allows families to balance fun and relaxation, while couples can enjoy intimate moments without feeling rushed. With its warm **Aloha Spirit**, stunning natural landscapes, and endless opportunities for adventure, Hawaii is a destination that creates memories to last a lifetime.

Pearl Harbor & USS Arizona Memorial (Oahu): A Journey Through History

The first time I visited **Pearl Harbor**, I wasn't prepared for the wave of emotions that would hit me the moment I stepped onto the memorial. I had read about the attack in history books, watched documentaries, and understood the significance of that day in 1941. But standing there, looking down at the wreckage of the **USS Arizona**, I felt something deeper—a connection to the past, to the lives lost, and to the weight of history that still lingers over the water.

As I rode the boat across the harbor, the once-bustling military base felt eerily still. The American flag waved above the water, and the only sounds were the soft lapping of waves and the murmurs of visitors absorbing the solemn atmosphere. When I stepped onto the **USS Arizona Memorial**, I looked down and saw the outline of the battleship, still resting where it sank over 80 years ago. The oil, known as the *Black Tears of the Arizona*, still seeped from the wreckage, a silent reminder of the tragedy that unfolded here.

Walking through the memorial, I saw the names of the **1,177 sailors and Marines** etched into the white marble walls. Many of them were barely out of their teens when they perished. There was a heaviness in the air, a quiet reverence among visitors, as if we all understood that this wasn't just a historical site—it was a sacred place where time had frozen on December 7, 1941.

Pearl Harbor is more than just a **museum or a tourist attraction**—it's a powerful, living reminder of the sacrifices made during World War II. In this chapter, we'll explore **the significance of Pearl Harbor, the must-visit sites within the historic complex, and how to make the most of your visit**. Whether you have a deep appreciation for history or simply want to honor those who came before us, this is a place that will leave a lasting impact, just as it did on me.

The Attack on Pearl Harbor: A Pivotal Moment in History

The morning of **December 7, 1941**, started like any other in **Pearl Harbor, Oahu**. The sun was rising over the calm waters of the Pacific, and thousands of U.S. Navy personnel were going about their routines. **Just before 8:00 AM, everything changed.** Without warning, waves of Japanese warplanes roared over the harbor, unleashing a devastating attack that would alter the course of history.

In just under two hours, **more than 2,400 Americans lost their lives**, and much of the U.S. Pacific Fleet was left in flames. **Five battleships were sunk or severely damaged**, with the **USS Arizona** suffering the worst fate—taking **1,177 sailors and Marines** down with her as she exploded and sank within minutes. The attack shocked the world and pushed the United States into **World War II**, a conflict that would rage on for another four years.

Standing at **Pearl Harbor today**, it's hard to imagine the chaos and destruction of that morning. The peaceful waters and blue skies contrast sharply with the images of burning ships and desperate sailors fighting for survival. Visiting **the memorials and museums here is not just about learning history—it's about stepping into a moment that changed the world.**

USS Arizona Memorial: A Symbol of Sacrifice

The **USS Arizona Memorial** is the most powerful and emotional site at **Pearl Harbor**. Floating directly above the sunken battleship, the memorial serves as the final resting place for those who perished on board.

Visiting the memorial begins with a short film that provides historical context, featuring rare footage from the attack. As you watch the events unfold, you can't help but feel the tension build. Then, a **U.S. Navy shuttle boat** transports visitors across the harbor to the white, solemn structure that straddles the submerged wreckage of the **Arizona**.

Once on the memorial, the reality of what happened here becomes impossible to ignore. Looking down into the water, the outline of the **Arizona** is still visible beneath the waves. Small droplets of oil, often called the **"Black Tears of the Arizona,"** still rise from the ship's hull, a haunting reminder that this battleship—and those entombed within it—will forever be part of Pearl Harbor's waters.

Inside the memorial, a marble wall bears the names of **all 1,177 sailors and Marines** who lost their lives when the ship exploded. The atmosphere is reverent, with visitors speaking in hushed tones, paying their respects to those who made the ultimate sacrifice. Some families of survivors have even chosen to have their remains placed inside the wreckage, allowing them to rest alongside their fallen shipmates.

The **USS Arizona Memorial is more than just a place of remembrance—it is a symbol of resilience, unity, and the cost of war.** No visit to Pearl Harbor is complete without experiencing its profound significance.

Battleship Missouri: The End of World War II

While the **USS Arizona Memorial** marks the beginning of America's involvement in World War II, the **Battleship Missouri (BB-63)** represents the war's end. Nicknamed **"Mighty Mo,"** this legendary battleship is where **Japan officially surrendered to the United States on September 2, 1945**, bringing an end to the deadliest conflict in human history.

Visitors can step aboard the **USS Missouri**, walking the same decks where General Douglas MacArthur and Japanese officials signed the **Instrument of Surrender**. The exact spot is marked with a plaque, allowing visitors to stand in the place where history was made.

Exploring the ship, it's easy to get a sense of what life was like for the sailors who served on board. From the **massive 16-inch guns** that could fire shells over 20 miles to the cramped sleeping quarters below deck, the **USS Missouri** offers a fascinating glimpse into naval warfare. Despite its imposing size and firepower, it's remembered not for battle, but for being the site where **peace was restored**.

Standing on the decks of **Mighty Mo**, with the **USS Arizona Memorial visible in the distance**, is a powerful moment. It reminds visitors that Pearl Harbor is not just a place of tragedy, but also of triumph and closure.

A Visit That Stays With You

Pearl Harbor is not just a historical site—it is a place that demands reflection. The **USS Arizona Memorial and Battleship Missouri** tell a story that stretches from the beginning of America's involvement in World War II to its final chapter. Walking these grounds, you don't just learn about history—you **feel it**.

Visiting these memorials is an experience that stays with you long after you leave. It's a sobering reminder of the cost of war, the bravery of those who served, and the importance of remembering the past. For anyone visiting Oahu, Pearl Harbor is a **must-see destination that provides one of the most profound and humbling experiences in all of Hawaii.**

Pacific Aviation Museum & Other Key Sites

While the **USS Arizona Memorial** and **Battleship Missouri** are the most well-known sites at Pearl Harbor, the **Pacific Aviation Museum** and several other key locations provide a deeper understanding of the attack and its impact on World War II. These sites bring history to life through restored aircraft, immersive exhibits, and stories of heroism that shaped the course of history.

Located on **Ford Island**, the **Pearl Harbor Aviation Museum** is housed in two historic hangars that still bear the scars of the December 7, 1941 attack. Walking through these hangars, you can see **bullet holes and damage** left by Japanese fighter planes during the assault, a chilling reminder of how suddenly war arrived on American soil. The museum's collection includes **vintage warplanes**, such as the iconic **P-40 Warhawk**, which was used by U.S. pilots in their desperate attempt to fight back against the attack.

One of the most impressive exhibits is the **B-17 Flying Fortress**, a massive bomber that played a crucial role in the Pacific theater. Standing next to it, you get a sense of the sheer scale of the aircraft used during World War II. Other highlights include a **Japanese Zero fighter**, one of the planes responsible for the destruction at Pearl Harbor, and an interactive flight simulator where visitors can experience what it was like to be a WWII pilot.

In addition to the **Aviation Museum**, visitors can explore **the USS Bowfin Submarine**, docked near the Pearl Harbor Visitor Center. Nicknamed **"The Pearl Harbor Avenger,"** this submarine was launched exactly one year after the attack and went on to complete nine successful war patrols. Touring the **tight corridors, torpedo rooms, and control center** gives visitors a firsthand look at the intense conditions submariners endured while fighting in the Pacific.

Pearl Harbor is also home to the **Pearl Harbor Visitor Center**, which serves as the starting point for most visits. The center offers a **wealth of historical information, personal stories from survivors, and detailed exhibits on the events leading up to and following the attack**. Before heading out to the memorials, visitors can watch an **emotional documentary featuring actual footage from December 7, 1941**, setting the stage for the powerful experiences ahead.

These sites add layers of depth to a Pearl Harbor visit, offering insight into the **aviation, naval, and personal stories that define this chapter in history**.

Guided Tours vs. Self-Guided Experience

When visiting Pearl Harbor, one of the biggest decisions travelers face is whether to **explore on their own** or **join a guided tour**. Both options offer distinct advantages, depending on what kind of experience you're looking for.

For those who **prefer flexibility**, a **self-guided tour** is the best option. Pearl Harbor's visitor center is well-organized, and with an **official audio guide**, visitors can explore at their own pace. Self-guided visits allow for **more personal reflection**, especially at the **USS Arizona Memorial**, where many prefer to spend time in quiet contemplation. Since the **USS Bowfin Submarine, Pacific Aviation Museum, and Battleship Missouri** each have their own unique exhibits, a self-paced visit ensures that you can **prioritize the areas that interest you the most**.

However, **navigating Pearl Harbor's different sites requires planning**. Ford Island, where the **Aviation Museum and Battleship Missouri** are located, is accessible only via a **shuttle bus** from the visitor center, which runs at specific times. Visitors should also reserve **USS Arizona Memorial tickets in advance**, as spaces fill up quickly.

For those who want **a more structured and immersive experience**, **guided tours** offer several advantages. Many tours include **historian-led insights**, providing in-depth storytelling and context that brings history to life. Guides often share **firsthand accounts, survivor stories, and lesser-known details**, enriching the overall experience.

Some guided tours also include **roundtrip transportation from Waikiki**, eliminating the hassle of driving and parking. Since Pearl Harbor is a **large and multi-site attraction**, having a guide can make it easier to navigate, ensuring that visitors **maximize their time** and don't miss any key exhibits.

Several **highly rated guided tours** include:
✔ **Half-day Pearl Harbor tours**, covering the **USS Arizona Memorial and the visitor center.**
✔ **Full-day WWII tours**, which include the **USS Missouri, USS Bowfin, and Pacific Aviation Museum.**
✔ **Private tours**, offering **a more personalized experience with a dedicated guide.**

For history buffs or those short on time, **a guided tour ensures a seamless experience with expert narration**. However, those who prefer **independent exploration and a slower pace** may find a **self-guided visit more rewarding**.

Best Time to Visit & Essential Tips

Pearl Harbor is one of Hawaii's most **visited attractions**, and planning ahead can make a huge difference in avoiding crowds and making the most of your visit.

The **best time to visit** Pearl Harbor is **early in the morning**, as soon as it opens at **7:00 AM**. Arriving early allows visitors to **secure a spot on one of the first boats to the USS Arizona Memorial**, which is typically less crowded and more peaceful. The **midday hours tend to be the busiest**, especially between **10:00 AM and 2:00 PM**, when large tour groups arrive.

If possible, visiting on a **weekday** is recommended, as **weekends and holidays** bring even larger crowds. The site is **open daily except on Thanksgiving, Christmas, and New Year's Day**.

To ensure a smooth experience, here are a few essential tips:

✔ **Reserve Tickets in Advance:** Tickets to the **USS Arizona Memorial** are **free**, but they must be **reserved online through the National Park Service website**. Spaces fill up quickly, so booking **weeks in advance** is highly recommended.

✔ **Arrive Early for Walk-Up Tickets:** If you couldn't reserve a ticket, a limited number of **same-day tickets** are available on a **first-come, first-served basis**. Arriving **before 7:00 AM** increases your chances of getting one.

✔ **Dress Respectfully:** Pearl Harbor is a **memorial site, not just a tourist attraction**. Visitors should wear **modest, respectful attire**—bathing suits, overly casual beachwear, or revealing clothing are discouraged.

✔ **Pack Light:** For security reasons, **bags, backpacks, and large purses are not allowed inside Pearl Harbor**. Lockers are available for a small fee, but to avoid the hassle, it's best to **carry only essentials like a phone, wallet, and camera**.

✔ **Plan for at Least 4–5 Hours:** Even if you only plan to visit the **USS Arizona Memorial**, expect to spend **a minimum of 3–4 hours** at Pearl Harbor. If visiting the **Missouri, Bowfin, and Aviation Museum**, plan for **a full-day experience**.

✔ **Stay Hydrated & Wear Sunscreen:** Much of Pearl Harbor is **outdoors**, and the Hawaiian sun can be intense. Bring **a refillable water bottle** and apply **reef-safe sunscreen** before your visit.

✔ **Take Time to Reflect:** Pearl Harbor is not just about history—it's a place of **remembrance and respect**. Many visitors find themselves deeply moved by the experience, so taking a moment to reflect at the **USS Arizona Memorial or the Remembrance Circle** is an essential part of the visit.

A trip to Pearl Harbor is more than just a historical excursion—it's **a journey through one of the most pivotal moments in world history**. Whether you choose a **guided tour or a self-paced visit**, experiencing **these memorials and museums firsthand** will leave a lasting impact, reminding us of the sacrifices made and the resilience of those who lived through that fateful day.

Haleakalā National Park (Maui): Witnessing the Sunrise Above the Clouds

I still remember the feeling of standing at the summit of **Haleakalā**, wrapped in layers of warmth, shivering slightly—not just from the cold, but from the anticipation. It was **3:30 AM**, and the only light came from the headlights of cars winding up the steep, dark road. The drive had been long and winding, climbing nearly **10,000 feet above sea level**, but as I stepped out of the car, the crisp mountain air jolted me awake.

As I found a spot along the crater's edge, the sky was a deep shade of navy, speckled with stars so bright it felt like I was floating in space. There was a quiet hum of conversation among other early risers, but mostly, there was silence—a stillness that made it clear this was a sacred place. Then, as the first golden rays broke over the horizon, **the world slowly transformed**. The sky exploded in hues of orange, pink, and purple, painting a masterpiece that no photograph could ever do justice. Below us, a vast sea of clouds stretched endlessly, making it feel like we were standing on the edge of heaven.

Watching the sunrise at **Haleakalā National Park** isn't just a bucket-list experience—it's something that stays with you long after you leave. It's a moment of **awe, reflection, and deep appreciation for nature's beauty**. In this chapter, we'll explore everything you need to know to **witness this breathtaking sunrise for yourself**—from **how to prepare for the journey** to **the best spots to take in the view**, ensuring you don't miss one of the most **unforgettable sights in Hawaii**.

The Iconic Haleakalā Sunrise & Sunset Experience

There are few places on Earth where you can witness a sunrise so breathtaking that it feels like a spiritual awakening. **Haleakalā National Park**, home to **Maui's highest peak at 10,023 feet**, offers one of the most **legendary sunrise experiences in the world**. The moment the first golden light spills over the horizon, illuminating the vast volcanic crater and the sea of clouds below, time seems to stand still.

The journey to the summit begins in the dead of night. Winding up the **steep, 37-mile road** from sea level, travelers make their way in near-total darkness, with only the glow of headlights cutting through the mist. The higher you climb, the more the temperature drops, and by the time you reach the summit, the tropical warmth of Maui's beaches feels like a distant memory. But as the sky begins to shift from deep midnight blue to soft shades of violet and pink, all discomfort fades. When the sun finally **breaks through the clouds**, lighting up the sky in shades of gold and crimson, there's an overwhelming sense of peace—a **moment of pure magic that no photograph can truly capture**.

While sunrise is **the most popular time to visit**, Haleakalā's **sunset experience** is equally mesmerizing and far less crowded. As the sun dips below the horizon, the crater is bathed in **deep purples, fiery oranges, and rich reds**, creating an otherworldly landscape that feels like the surface of Mars. **After dark, Haleakalā transforms into one of the world's best stargazing locations**, with **zero light pollution and a night sky bursting with constellations, planets, and even the Milky Way.**

Whether you visit at sunrise, sunset, or under the stars, **Haleakalā is more than just a scenic spot—it's a humbling and unforgettable experience**.

Top Hiking Trails: Sliding Sands & Halemauʻu Trail

Haleakalā isn't just about the sunrise—it's also a **hiker's paradise**, offering some of the most unique and otherworldly landscapes in Hawaii. Within the vast **Haleakalā Crater**, trails wind through **lava rock fields, cinder cones, and rolling sand dunes**, creating an environment that feels closer to the surface of Mars than a tropical island.

The two most famous trails—**Sliding Sands (Keonehe'ehe'e Trail)** and **Halemauʻu Trail**—offer vastly different perspectives of the **volcanic landscape** and are must-dos for adventurous visitors.

Sliding Sands Trail (Keoneheʻeheʻe Trail) – The Crater Descent

This **challenging** yet **breathtaking** trail begins right at the **Haleakalā Summit** and descends **into the heart of the crater**, offering a **front-row seat to Haleakalā's lunar-like terrain**. As you hike down, the landscape shifts dramatically, from **dark volcanic rock fields to rolling red and orange dunes**, and past **ancient cinder cones that rise like miniature volcanoes**.

Though the **views are unparalleled**, this hike is **not for the faint of heart**. What makes Sliding Sands unique is the **reverse difficulty**—it's **easy going down**, but brutal coming back up. The elevation gain, thin air, and loose sand make the **return hike incredibly strenuous**, so many hikers opt to **hike halfway down and turn back** rather than complete the full **11-mile round-trip trek**.

For those looking for **an unforgettable one-way hike**, some visitors combine Sliding Sands with **Halemauʻu Trail** (with a pre-arranged shuttle), descending into the crater via **Sliding Sands** and exiting through the **Halemauʻu switchbacks**.

Halemauʻu Trail – The Cliffside Views

Unlike Sliding Sands, which starts at the summit, **Halemauʻu Trail** begins **at a lower elevation** and provides a **more gradual descent** into the crater. What makes this trail spectacular is its **dramatic, panoramic views** of the crater from above. The **switchback section near the crater rim** is particularly breathtaking, offering jaw-dropping **cliffside vistas** that rival any scenic overlook in the park.

Hikers on **Halemauʻu Trail** get to experience a mix of **lush greenery, misty clouds rolling in over the cliffs, and barren volcanic terrain**—a stark contrast that showcases **Haleakalā's diverse ecosystem**. While the full trail is **8 miles round trip**, many hikers choose to do a **shorter version to the crater overlook (about 2.5 miles round trip)**, which still delivers unforgettable views.

Both **Sliding Sands and Halemauʻu** offer a chance to truly immerse yourself in **Haleakalā's raw beauty**, but they require careful planning. With **elevation changes, unpredictable weather, and challenging terrain**, it's important to **bring plenty of water, wear layers, and pace yourself**.

Whether you're watching the **sunrise from the summit** or **hiking into the crater's depths**, **Haleakalā National Park is one of Maui's most extraordinary experiences**—one that leaves visitors in awe of nature's power and beauty.

Rare Wildlife & Native Hawaiian Culture

Haleakalā National Park isn't just a place of dramatic landscapes and breathtaking sunrises—it's also home to some of **Hawaii's rarest wildlife** and holds deep cultural significance for Native Hawaiians. The park's diverse ecosystems, ranging from **lush rainforests to barren volcanic landscapes**, provide sanctuary for endangered species found nowhere else in the world.

One of the most **iconic and rare birds** within the park is the ʻāpalephe **(Hawaiian honeycreeper)**, a brightly colored, nectar-feeding bird that flits through the park's native forests. Even more elusive is the **nēnē (Hawaiian goose)**, Hawaii's state bird, which was once on the brink of extinction. Thanks to conservation efforts, visitors today may spot **nēnē foraging in the grassy areas of Haleakalā's slopes**. Seeing these birds in their natural habitat is a reminder of Hawaii's delicate ecosystem and the efforts being made to preserve it.

Perhaps the most fascinating plant found at Haleakalā is the **silversword (ʻāhinahina)**, a rare, otherworldly-looking species that thrives in the harsh volcanic environment. This **silvery, spiky-leafed plant** can live for up to **50 years** before blooming once in its lifetime, producing a spectacular tall stalk of purple flowers before dying. The silversword is found **only in high-altitude regions of Maui's Haleakalā and the Big Island's Mauna Kea**, making it one of the rarest plant species in the world.

Beyond its wildlife, Haleakalā is deeply woven into **Hawaiian mythology and cultural traditions**. The name **Haleakalā** means **"House of the Sun"** in Hawaiian, and according to legend, the demigod **Maui** lassoed the sun from the summit, slowing its journey across the sky so that daylight would last longer. This sacred site was once a place where Hawaiian priests (kahuna) performed **ceremonies and rituals**, and even today, Native Hawaiian cultural practitioners continue to visit the summit for spiritual practices. Visitors are encouraged to respect the land, follow park guidelines, and appreciate **Haleakalā's significance beyond just its beauty—it is a place of deep ancestral connection.**

Stargazing at the Summit: One of the Best in the World

As breathtaking as Haleakalā is at sunrise and sunset, **its magic doesn't end when the sun goes down**. At night, the summit transforms into **one of the best stargazing locations in the world**, offering an unparalleled view of the cosmos. With **zero light pollution and a high-altitude vantage point**, Haleakalā provides a front-row seat to the **Milky Way, distant planets, and endless constellations**.

On a clear night, the sky explodes with thousands of stars, and on particularly dark nights, you can even see the **Andromeda Galaxy with the naked eye**. The thin, dry air at Haleakalā's summit makes for some of the **clearest skies on Earth**, and astronomers from around the world consider it **one of the best stargazing locations in the entire Pacific**.

For those who want to enhance their experience, several **stargazing tours** are available, led by expert astronomers who provide telescopes and guide visitors through the celestial wonders above. The **University of Hawaii's Haleakalā Observatory**, located near the summit, is a world-renowned research facility that studies everything from space debris to deep-space objects. While the observatory is not open to the public, visitors can still admire the massive telescopes and scientific equipment that sit atop the peak.

Even without a telescope, **simply laying back and looking up at the night sky is an unforgettable experience**. The best stargazing conditions are on **moonless nights**, so checking the lunar calendar before planning a visit is recommended. Whether you come for the **sunrise, the sunset, or the stars**, Haleakalā's summit offers a celestial experience unlike any other.

What to Pack & How to Prepare for the Altitude

Visiting Haleakalā may feel like stepping into another world, but that world comes with extreme conditions that require careful preparation. The summit's **high altitude, unpredictable weather, and dramatic temperature shifts** make it essential to **pack smart and be aware of how the elevation affects the body**.

Dressing for the Cold

One of the biggest surprises for many visitors is **just how cold it gets at the summit**. Despite being on a tropical island, temperatures at **10,000 feet** can drop below freezing, especially at sunrise and after dark.

✔ **Layered clothing** – A **warm fleece or down jacket, gloves, and a hat** are essential for staying comfortable.

✔ **Windproof outer layer** – The summit is often **extremely windy**, so bringing a **windbreaker or rain jacket** is a good idea.
✔ **Closed-toe shoes** – Hiking boots or sturdy sneakers are recommended, as the terrain can be rocky and uneven.

Dealing with High Altitude

At **10,023 feet**, the air at Haleakalā is **thin and contains less oxygen**, which can cause altitude sickness in some visitors. Symptoms can include **dizziness, headaches, nausea, and shortness of breath**.

✔ **Stay hydrated** – Drink plenty of water before and during your visit to help combat altitude effects.
✔ **Take it slow** – If you feel lightheaded, avoid sudden movements and take deep breaths.
✔ **Consider altitude medication** – If you're prone to altitude sickness, consult a doctor about potential preventative medications.

Essentials to Bring

✔ **Sunscreen & sunglasses** – The high elevation means **strong UV exposure**, even on cloudy days.
✔ **Snacks & water** – There are **no food or drink options at the summit**, so bringing your own is necessary.
✔ **Camera & tripod** – Whether capturing the **sunrise, sunset, or stars**, a tripod is helpful for stable, long-exposure shots.

✔ **Reserve your sunrise spot in advance** – The **Haleakalā Sunrise Permit** must be booked online through the **National Park Service website**.
✔ **Arrive early** – Parking fills up fast, and the best sunrise viewing spots go quickly.
✔ **Be mindful of local customs** – Haleakalā is **a sacred place**, so visitors should be **respectful and avoid loud conversations or disruptive behavior**.

A trip to Haleakalā is a **once-in-a-lifetime experience**, but it requires careful planning to **ensure safety and comfort**. Whether you're **marveling at the rare silversword plants, standing in awe of the Milky Way, or watching the first light of day spill over the clouds, Haleakalā is a place that reminds us just how powerful and beautiful nature can be.**

Hawai'i Volcanoes National Park (Big Island): The Land of Fire and Lava

I still remember the moment I first saw the **glow of molten lava** against the night sky, a fiery ribbon of orange and red cutting through the darkness. The air was thick with the scent of sulfur, and the heat radiating from the distant lava flows was almost surreal. Standing on the **hardened black lava fields**, I felt like I had stepped onto another planet—one shaped not by time, but by the raw power of the Earth itself.

Visiting **Hawai'i Volcanoes National Park** is unlike anything else in Hawaii. While the islands are famous for their beaches, waterfalls, and lush rainforests, **this place is pure, untamed energy**—a reminder that Hawaii is still **alive and constantly evolving**. This is where **land is still being created**, where the forces of nature are on full display, and where the legend of Pele, the Hawaiian goddess of fire and volcanoes, feels more real than ever.

I remember hiking across the vast **Kīlauea Iki Crater**, where a lava lake once boiled in the 1959 eruption. The ground beneath my feet, though solid, still held the echoes of that explosion. Steam vents hissed as I passed, releasing whispers of heat from deep within the

Earth. Later, at **Halemaʻumaʻu Crater**, I stood at the rim and watched as thick plumes of volcanic gas drifted into the sky, a constant reminder that **Kīlauea, one of the most active volcanoes in the world, is still very much alive**.

Hawaiʻi Volcanoes National Park isn't just about watching lava—it's about **witnessing the Earth in motion**, understanding the power that shaped these islands, and feeling an almost spiritual connection to the forces that have both destroyed and created life here for centuries. Whether you're **hiking across lava fields, exploring lava tubes, or standing at the edge of a crater**, this park offers an experience that is humbling, mesmerizing, and unforgettable.

In this chapter, we'll explore everything you need to know about **visiting this awe-inspiring national park**—from the **best trails and viewpoints** to the **safest ways to witness active lava flows**, ensuring that your journey into the **Land of Fire and Lava** is one you'll never forget.

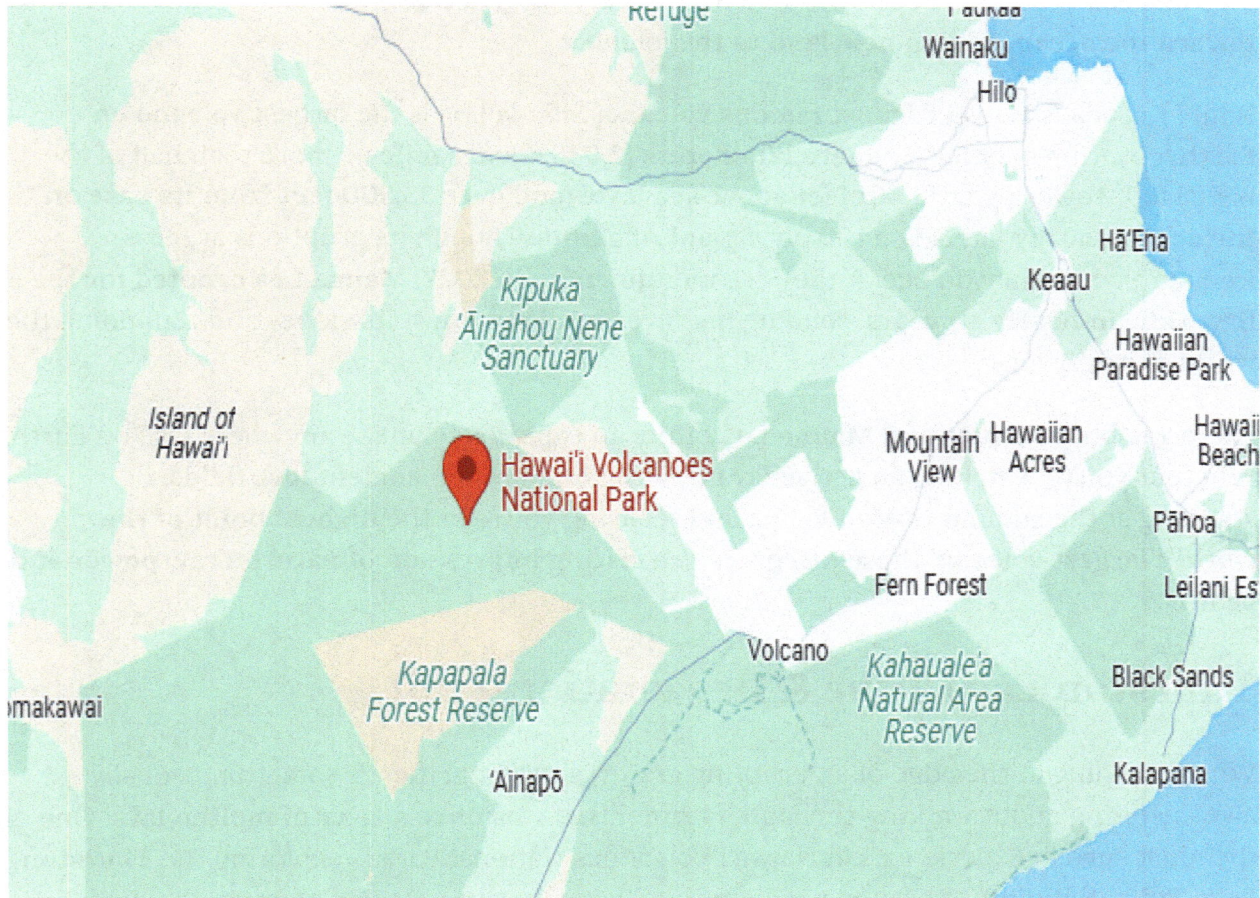

Kīlauea & Mauna Loa: Exploring Hawaii's Active Volcanoes

Hawaiʻi Volcanoes National Park is home to two of the most **powerful and legendary volcanoes in the world—Kīlauea and Mauna Loa**. These giants have shaped the Hawaiian landscape for millions of years, creating vast lava fields, rugged coastlines, and one of the most **geologically dynamic regions on the planet**. Unlike dormant or extinct volcanoes, these two remain **active, alive, and constantly reshaping the land**.

Standing at the **rim of Kīlauea's Halemaʻumaʻu Crater**, I could feel the heat rising from the Earth itself. The air smelled of sulfur, and plumes of steam and volcanic gases swirled upward into the sky. It was hard to comprehend that beneath my feet, a massive reservoir of molten rock was churning, occasionally forcing its way to the surface in spectacular eruptions. **Kīlauea has been one of the most active volcanoes in the world for centuries**, erupting as recently as 2023, often with **slow-moving lava flows that creep down its flanks toward the ocean, adding new land to the island**.

While Kīlauea is **Hawaiʻi's most famous volcano**, Mauna Loa is the **largest volcano on Earth**, covering over **5,271 square kilometers (2,035 square miles)**—more than half of the Big Island. Towering at **13,681 feet above sea level (and over 33,500 feet from its base on the ocean floor),** Mauna Loa is truly a **giant of giants**. Though its eruptions are less frequent, when they do occur, they are **monumental**. In **2022, Mauna Loa erupted for the first time in nearly 40 years**, sending massive lava flows down its slopes and reminding the world of its power.

Exploring both **Kīlauea and Mauna Loa** offers an experience unlike anywhere else on Earth. Whether you're watching an **active lava flow**, hiking through **ancient lava fields**, or standing at the summit of Mauna Loa and realizing you're at the **highest point of the world's largest volcano**, these places leave a **lasting impression of nature's raw power and beauty**.

Thurston Lava Tube & Devastation Trail

While standing at the edge of an erupting crater is thrilling, there's something equally awe-inspiring about **walking through a tunnel that was once a river of molten lava**. One of the most surreal experiences in Hawaiʻi Volcanoes National Park is exploring the **Thurston Lava Tube (Nāhuku)**—a natural tunnel formed when **hot lava flowed beneath the surface and later drained away, leaving behind a hollow cave-like structure**.

The **entrance to the lava tube feels like stepping into a prehistoric world**, surrounded by towering ferns, dripping moss, and dense rainforest. Inside, the tunnel stretches **600 feet**, with smooth, solidified lava walls that once carried **a river of fire**. As I walked through, I imagined the molten rock rushing through the tube centuries ago, carving out this incredible passageway. The air inside was cool and damp—a stark contrast to the fiery process that created it. At night, when the lights are turned off, the cave is **completely pitch black**, offering a sense of what early Hawaiians must have felt as they explored these volcanic tunnels.

A short drive from the lava tube brings visitors to another must-see location: **Devastation Trail**. This eerie landscape is a stark reminder of what happens when the power of a volcano meets lush vegetation. Formed by **Kīlauea's violent 1959 eruption**, this barren, **ash-covered expanse was once a thriving rainforest**, completely wiped out by a massive lava fountain that reached over **1,900 feet into the air**. Walking along the trail, the contrast is striking—**charred tree stumps stand frozen in time**, surrounded by an otherworldly terrain of volcanic cinders. Yet, even here, life is returning—small green plants have begun sprouting from the ash, showing the resilience of nature.

Both **Thurston Lava Tube and Devastation Trail** provide a **deeper understanding of the life cycle of a volcano**—from its destructive force to the way it eventually nurtures new growth. These sites remind us that **Hawai'i is a land in constant motion, a place where the past, present, and future of the Earth's geology are unfolding before our eyes.**

Chain of Craters Road & Lava Viewing Areas

Driving down **Chain of Craters Road** feels like stepping into a **prehistoric world where Earth is still being shaped**. This **19-mile scenic route** winds from the **Kīlauea Caldera** down to the Pacific coastline, cutting through vast lava fields, crumbling sea cliffs, and remnants of communities that were buried by past eruptions. Every twist and turn along the way reveals a different side of **Hawai'i Volcanoes National Park**, from **ancient petroglyphs carved into hardened lava** to **recent lava flows that have reshaped the land.**

As I drove along the **steep descent toward the coast**, I couldn't help but be mesmerized by the landscape. Fields of **solidified lava stretched endlessly in every direction**, some **smooth and ropy (pāhoehoe lava), others jagged and rough ('a'ā lava)**. The contrast between the black rock and the deep blue of the ocean created an **otherworldly beauty** that was both haunting and breathtaking.

At the end of the road, where the pavement abruptly stops, lies one of the most **dramatic scenes in the park**—the place where **lava once flowed directly into the ocean**, creating **billowing clouds of steam and new land formations**. While active ocean-entry lava flows aren't always present, when they do occur, **witnessing red-hot lava meeting the sea is one of the most powerful sights on Earth**. Even when lava isn't flowing into the ocean, the **hardened lava deltas and collapsed sea cliffs** tell the story of past eruptions, showing just how fragile and dynamic this land is.

For those seeking **lava viewing opportunities**, the experience depends entirely on Kīlauea's activity at the time. Some years, lava **flows freely from vents**, creating glowing rivers of molten rock that can be seen from safe observation areas. Other times, lava **remains confined within Halemaʻumaʻu Crater**, visible only as an **inner glow reflecting against volcanic gases at night**. The best way to check for **current lava activity** is to visit the **Hawaiʻi Volcanoes National Park website** or speak with park rangers upon arrival.

Regardless of whether lava is flowing, Chain of Craters Road remains a **must-visit**—a journey through time, where the Earth's raw energy is on full display.

Cultural & Geological Significance of the Park

Hawaiʻi Volcanoes National Park isn't just a **natural wonder—it's a sacred place deeply intertwined with Native Hawaiian culture and legends**. The park is home to **Pele, the Hawaiian goddess of fire, lightning, and volcanoes**, who is believed to **reside within Halemaʻumaʻu Crater**. According to Hawaiian tradition, Pele's **fiery temper and creative force** are responsible for shaping the islands, and her presence is still felt throughout the volcanic landscape. Many Hawaiians offer **hoʻokupu (gifts)** to Pele, such as ti leaves or Hawaiian salt, as a sign of respect.

One of the most **spiritually significant sites** in the park is **Puʻu Loa Petroglyphs**, located off Chain of Craters Road. Here, more than **23,000 ancient carvings are etched into the hardened lava**, depicting symbols of **birth, travel, and spiritual guidance**. These markings, made by Native Hawaiians centuries ago, serve as a reminder that this land has been **inhabited and honored long before it became a national park**.

Geologically, Hawaiʻi Volcanoes National Park is a **living laboratory of Earth's creation**. Mauna Loa and Kīlauea are **shield volcanoes**, formed by countless eruptions that have built up layer upon layer of lava rock. Kīlauea is **one of the most studied volcanoes in the world**, helping scientists understand how magma moves beneath the Earth's surface. Each eruption reshapes the land, adding new rock formations, creating **lava tubes**, and even altering coastlines as new land emerges from the sea.

This delicate balance between **destruction and creation, culture and science**, makes Hawaiʻi Volcanoes National Park one of the most unique places on Earth. Visitors are encouraged to **respect the land, listen to its stories, and appreciate the power of nature unfolding before their eyes.**

Safety Precautions & Best Visiting Seasons

Visiting an **active volcanic landscape** comes with certain risks, but with proper planning and awareness, it can be **a safe and unforgettable experience.** Hawai'i Volcanoes National Park is **constantly changing**, and conditions can shift rapidly due to **new lava flows, earthquakes, and volcanic gas emissions.**

Safety Tips for Exploring the Park

✔ **Stay on designated trails and viewing areas** – Lava fields can be **unstable and sharp,** and some areas have **hidden cracks or weak crusts** that can collapse underfoot.

✔ **Be aware of volcanic gases (vog)** – Kīlauea releases **sulfur dioxide gas**, which can cause **breathing difficulties, especially for those with asthma.** Check air quality conditions before heading to crater viewpoints.

✔ **Respect closures and warnings** – The National Park Service constantly **monitors volcanic activity,** and **restricted areas exist for a reason.** Entering closed zones can be **extremely dangerous.**

✔ **Bring plenty of water and snacks** – The park covers a vast area with **few facilities,** and dehydration is a serious concern, especially when hiking.

✔ **Wear sturdy shoes** – Walking on hardened lava **requires good traction**, as the surface can be sharp, uneven, and jagged. Flip-flops and sandals are not recommended.

✔ **Be prepared for unpredictable weather** – The park spans from **sea level to 13,681 feet,** meaning **temperatures and conditions vary drastically. Fog, rain, and strong winds** can arrive suddenly, so layering up is key.

Best Time to Visit

Hawai'i Volcanoes National Park is **open year-round,** but the best time to visit depends on **weather, crowd levels, and lava activity.**

- **Spring (March–May) & Fall (September–November)** – These are the **best months** to visit, with **fewer crowds, mild temperatures, and drier conditions.**
- **Winter (December–February)** – The park sees more **rainfall**, especially at higher elevations, but this can also bring **dramatic clouds and misty views over the crater.** Crowds are **higher around the holidays.**
- **Summer (June–August)** – This is the **busiest season,** with more visitors and **hotter temperatures** at lower elevations. However, summer also offers **clearer skies for lava viewing and stargazing.**

For those hoping to see **active lava flows**, there is **no guaranteed season**—Kīlauea's activity is unpredictable and changes frequently. The best way to **increase your chances of seeing lava** is to **monitor eruption reports** on the **Hawai'i Volcanoes National Park website** and visit **Halema'uma'u Crater after dark**, when lava glow (if present) is most visible.

Regardless of the season, **visiting Hawai'i Volcanoes National Park is an experience like no other**. Whether you're **driving Chain of Craters Road, hiking across a solidified lava lake, or witnessing Pele's fire in real-time**, this park is a place where **the Earth's past, present, and future unfold before your eyes**. It is a reminder of **both nature's destructive power and its incredible ability to create something new**.

Nā Pali Coast (Kauai): The Crown Jewel of Hawaii's Natural Beauty

The first time I saw the Nā Pali Coast, I felt like I had stepped into another world. Towering cliffs covered in lush greenery rose straight from the ocean, stretching as far as the eye could see. Waterfalls cascaded down sheer rock faces, disappearing into the turquoise waves below. There were no roads, no buildings—just pure, untouched wilderness. It was the kind of beauty that didn't just take your breath away, it made you feel small in the best possible way.

I first explored Nā Pali from the deck of a boat, sailing along the rugged coastline as the waves crashed against the cliffs. The wind carried the scent of salt and tropical flowers, and every turn revealed something new—a hidden cove, a massive sea cave, a pod of dolphins playing in the surf. As the sun dipped lower, the cliffs turned golden, and I knew I was witnessing something truly special.

Another day, I experienced Nā Pali from the air, soaring above the coastline in a small helicopter. From that perspective, I could see how remote and untouched this place truly was. Valleys carved deep into the island's heart, with rivers snaking through dense rainforests. In the distance, waterfalls tumbled from the highest peaks, feeding streams that had been flowing for centuries.

For the most immersive experience, I set out on the Kalalau Trail, the legendary footpath that winds along the cliffs. Hiking through dense jungle, crossing streams, and navigating steep ridges, I felt a deep connection to the land. This was once home to ancient Hawaiian communities, who lived off the rich resources of the valleys and the sea. Walking the same path they once traveled, I couldn't help but wonder what life must have been like here before the modern world arrived.

Nā Pali is more than just a beautiful place—it's a reminder of how wild and powerful nature can be. Whether you explore it by boat, helicopter, or on foot, it leaves a lasting impression. There are few places left in the world that feel this untouched, this sacred, and this awe-inspiring. Visiting Nā Pali isn't just about seeing a beautiful coastline—it's about experiencing a part of Hawaii that has remained unchanged for generations.

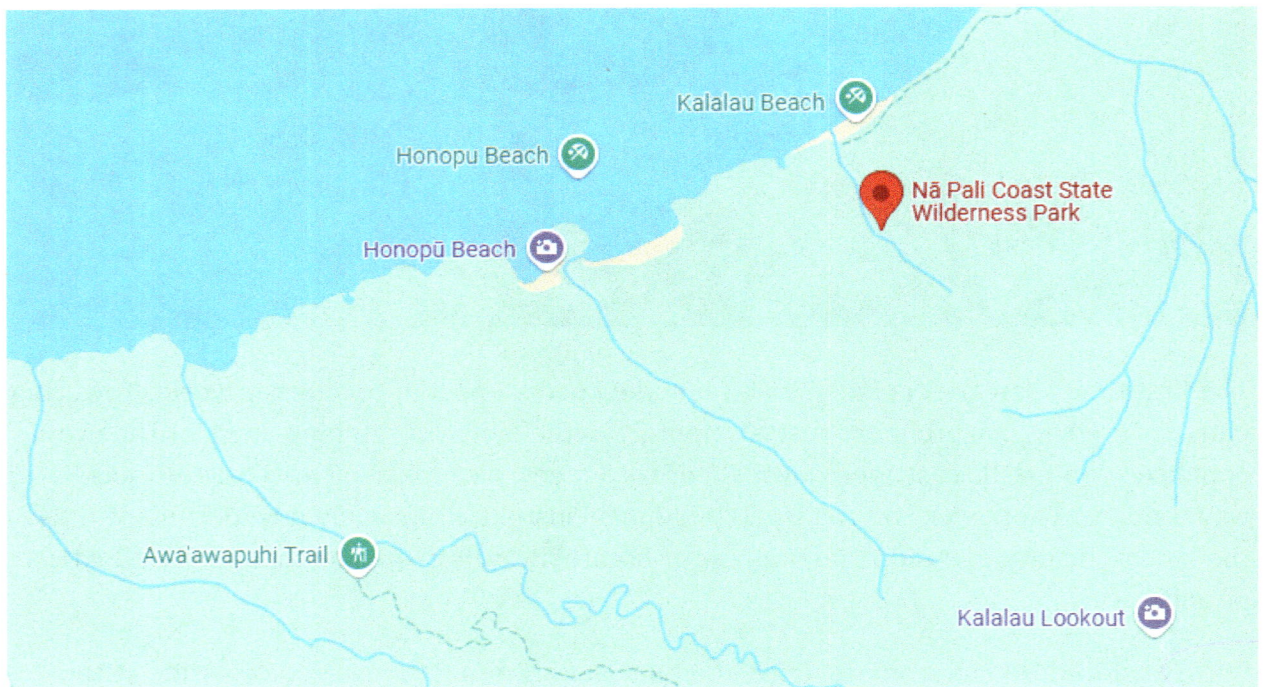

Scenic Helicopter & Boat Tours for Unmatched Views

Seeing the **Nā Pali Coast** from land is breathtaking, but nothing compares to the **unmatched views from a helicopter or boat**. Since the coastline is completely inaccessible by road, these two options offer the **best way to experience its dramatic cliffs, hidden beaches, and cascading waterfalls.**

A **helicopter tour** over Nā Pali is one of the most **unforgettable experiences in Hawaii.** From the air, the full scale of the coastline becomes clear—**3,000-foot cliffs rising straight from the ocean, deep emerald valleys carved by ancient rivers, and waterfalls spilling down rocky ledges into the sea.** As the helicopter glides through the mist, the perspective shifts, revealing untouched landscapes that few ever get to see. Flying into **Manawaiopuna Falls**, made famous by *Jurassic Park*, adds to the magic, while sweeping views of **Honopū Valley and Kalalau Beach** showcase the sheer beauty of this remote paradise.

For those who prefer to stay closer to the water, **boat tours offer an incredible way to explore Nā Pali from below.** Departing from **Hanalei or Port Allen**, these tours take visitors along the coast, weaving through **towering sea caves, past hidden coves, and along sheer cliffs** that seem to defy gravity. The ocean here is teeming with life—**spinner dolphins often ride alongside the boat, Hawaiian monk seals bask on rocky shores, and, during the winter months, humpback whales breach in the distance.** The most breathtaking moment comes when the sun begins to set, casting the cliffs in **golden light and painting the sky in shades of orange and pink.**

For the ultimate adventure, some boat tours offer **snorkeling excursions**, stopping in crystal-clear waters near **Nualolo Kai, an ancient Hawaiian fishing village.** Here, visitors can explore vibrant coral reefs, home to **colorful tropical fish, sea turtles, and even the occasional reef shark.**

Whether by **air or sea, experiencing Nā Pali from these unique perspectives is a must.** Each method offers something different—**helicopter tours provide breathtaking panoramic views, while boat tours allow for a more immersive experience with the ocean and marine life.** Choosing between the two is difficult, but if possible, experiencing both will provide the most complete and awe-inspiring view of this untouched paradise.

Hiking the Kalalau Trail: A Trekker's Paradise

For those who prefer to explore Nā Pali **on foot**, the **Kalalau Trail** offers one of the **most challenging yet rewarding hikes in the world**. This **11-mile trek** winds along the rugged coastline, cutting through **dense rainforests, steep ridges, and hidden valleys**, offering **breathtaking views at every turn**.

The **first two miles** from **Keʻe Beach to Hanakāpīʻai Beach** are the most popular and accessible section of the trail, perfect for those looking for a **short yet stunning hike**. This portion features **lush jungle paths, dramatic ocean views, and a golden-sand beach** at the end. However, Hanakāpīʻai Beach can be extremely dangerous for swimming, as its currents are notoriously strong.

Beyond this point, the trail becomes significantly **more difficult and remote**. The **full 11-mile trek to Kalalau Beach** is not for the faint of heart—it involves **steep cliffs, narrow switchbacks, river crossings, and rugged terrain**. But for those who make the journey, the reward is unlike anything else in Hawaii.

Reaching **Kalalau Beach** feels like stepping into a lost paradise. **Towering cliffs frame a secluded, crescent-shaped shoreline**, where the only sounds are the crashing waves and the wind rustling through the valley. The remoteness of this beach makes it **one of the most breathtaking and peaceful places in the world**.

Since the full hike requires a **permit and camping gear**, most visitors opt for a **day hike to Hanakāpīʻai Beach or Hanakāpīʻai Falls**, which is an **8-mile round trip** and features a **stunning 300-foot waterfall tucked deep within the rainforest**.

The **Kalalau Trail is as challenging as it is rewarding**, offering an experience that few other places on Earth can match. For experienced hikers looking for an **unparalleled adventure**, this trek provides **a true immersion into the raw, untouched beauty of the Nā Pali Coast**.

Secret Waterfalls and Hidden Beaches: Finding Nā Pali's Hidden Gems

Nā Pali's tall cliffs hide beautiful secrets. There are secluded beaches, mostly reached by boat or tough hikes, and waterfalls that cascade down the green cliffs. These hidden spots are a chance to experience Nā Pali's magic without the big crowds.

- **Hanakoa Falls:** Getting to Hanakoa Falls is a real adventure. It's a long, challenging 17-mile hike (there and back) on the Kalalau Trail. The waterfall itself is stunning, with two levels falling into a pool where you can cool off. The hike takes you through beautiful valleys with amazing coastal views. *Important: This hike is hard! You need to be prepared.*
- **Hanakapi'ai Beach:** You can reach Hanakapi'ai Beach by hiking the first two miles of the Kalalau Trail. It's a lovely beach at the start of the Hanakapi'ai Valley. *Warning: The ocean currents here are very strong, making swimming dangerous, especially in the winter.*
- **Kalalau Beach:** Kalalau Beach is at the very end of the Kalalau Trail. It's like a remote paradise, with golden sand, blue water, and huge cliffs behind it. You can camp here if you get a permit, which is an amazing experience. *Heads up: Permits are hard to get, so you have to book them way in advance.*
- **Hidden Coves and Sea Caves:** Boat tours and kayaking trips often visit hidden coves and sea caves along Nā Pali. This is a fantastic way to see secret beaches and waterfalls that you can't reach by land. You'll get to see the coastline from a unique perspective.

Kayaking and Snorkeling: Getting Up Close with Nā Pali

Paddling along the bottom of the huge cliffs gives you a close-up view of just how grand Nā Pali is. Kayaking and snorkeling tours let you explore hidden coves, paddle through sea caves, and see the colorful fish and other sea creatures that live here.

- **Kayaking Tours:** Lots of companies offer guided kayak tours along Nā Pali. You can choose from short half-day trips to longer multi-day adventures. *Pro Tip: Morning tours are usually better because the water is calmer, and you can see more clearly.*
- **Snorkeling:** The water around Nā Pali is so clear, it's perfect for snorkeling. You might see bright fish, sea turtles, and even monk seals! Many kayak tours include time for snorkeling in quiet coves.
- **Being Respectful:** When you're kayaking and snorkeling, remember that this is a delicate environment. Don't touch the coral, bother the sea animals, or leave any trash behind.

Best Photo Spots and Planning Your Trip: Capturing Nā Pali's Beauty

Nā Pali is a dream come true for photographers. The dramatic cliffs, waterfalls, and colorful sunsets give you tons of chances to take amazing pictures.

- **Kalalau Lookout:** This is an easy-to-reach viewpoint with wide-open views of Nā Pali. It's a great spot for sunset photos.
- **Waimea Canyon Drive:** There are several viewpoints along Waimea Canyon Drive that offer stunning views of Nā Pali from above.
- **Boat Tours:** Boat tours give you unique photo opportunities, showing you the coastline from the water.
- **Helicopter Tours:** If you want a truly unforgettable experience, try a helicopter tour. The views of Nā Pali from the air are incredible.
- **Planning Your Trip:** Nā Pali is a popular place, so it's important to plan ahead. If you want to hike the Kalalau Trail, you'll need permits, and they get booked up quickly. Boat tours and kayak trips also fill up fast, especially during the busy season. Think about what time of year you're going because the weather can affect whether you can get there.

Respecting the Culture and Nature:

Nā Pali is not just a beautiful place; it's also important to Native Hawaiians. Be respectful of the land, its history, and local traditions. Follow "Leave No Trace" rules – pack out everything you pack in, and be careful around sensitive areas.

Nā Pali is more than just a place to visit; it's an experience you'll never forget. Whether you hike its trails, paddle its waters, or just admire its beauty from a distance, the magic of Nā Pali will stay with you.

The Road to Hana (Maui): More Than Just a Drive – It's an Adventure

I'll never forget the morning I started my adventure on the Road to Hana. I was sitting on the balcony of my rental, sipping a warm cup of Hawaiian coffee, while the sunrise painted the sky with streaks of gold and pink. The excitement I felt was unmatched because I had heard so much about this famous drive, known for its beauty, charm, and the sense of adventure it brings.

With a map in one hand, snacks in my bag, and a playlist of Hawaiian music ready to go, I couldn't wait to explore the winding roads, lush forests, waterfalls, and beaches. The Road to Hana isn't just a drive; it's an unforgettable journey that shows you some of the most incredible sights on the island of Maui.

Must-Visit Stops Along the Way

The Road to Hana has so many amazing stops that you'll want to plan ahead. From breathtaking waterfalls to serene forests and unique beaches, here are some of the highlights you shouldn't miss:

Twin Falls (Mile Marker 2)
One of the first stops is Twin Falls, where you can take a short, easy hike through tropical greenery to see not just one but two beautiful waterfalls. If it's a hot day, you can even take a swim in the pools beneath the falls. Don't forget to stop at the small fruit stand nearby to grab fresh coconut water, smoothies, or banana bread for the road.

Black Sand Beach (Waiʻānapanapa State Park)
Waiʻānapanapa State Park is famous for its striking black sand beach, formed from volcanic rock. The beach is stunning, with its dark sand and bright blue waves creating a picture-perfect scene. This park also has sea caves, lava tubes, and trails for hiking. Take your time here to explore and soak in the beauty.

Bamboo Forest (Pipiwai Trail)
If you've ever wanted to walk through a magical bamboo forest, the Pipiwai Trail is the place to do it. As you stroll along the trail, the tall bamboo stalks sway gently above you, creating a peaceful and otherworldly atmosphere. It's one of the most unique places along the Road to Hana and worth every step.

Waterfalls to Marvel At

The Road to Hana is known for its waterfalls, and each one is special in its own way.

Wailua Falls (Mile Marker 45)
 This breathtaking waterfall is one of the tallest and most powerful on the island. It plunges 80 feet into a serene pool below. You can see it right from the road, but if you visit early in the morning, you'll have a better chance of enjoying it without too many other people around.

Ohe'o Gulch (Seven Sacred Pools)
 Located in Haleakalā National Park, the Seven Sacred Pools are a series of waterfalls and natural pools surrounded by lush greenery. You can take a dip in the pools or just enjoy the scenery. Make sure to check weather conditions because heavy rains can make swimming unsafe.

Hidden Gems and Local Stops

While the popular spots are amazing, the Road to Hana is full of surprises.

Waianapanapa Caves
 Within Wai'ānapanapa State Park, you'll find mysterious caves that feel like stepping into an ancient world. The caves are part of Hawaiian folklore and have a calm, almost haunting beauty.

Ke'anae Blowhole
 This blowhole on the Ke'anae Peninsula is a natural spectacle where ocean waves crash against lava rock, shooting water high into the air. It's thrilling to watch and makes for great photos.

Local Food Stops
 You can't drive the Road to Hana without tasting some local treats. Aunty Sandy's Banana Bread is famous for its warm, freshly baked banana bread—perfect for snacking as you explore. Hana Farms is another must-stop spot for fresh tropical fruit, homemade jams, and taro chips.

Should You Drive Yourself or Take a Guided Tour?

The Road to Hana offers two ways to experience its beauty:

- **Drive Yourself**: If you love exploring at your own pace and enjoy making unplanned stops, self-driving is the way to go. Just be prepared for narrow roads, sharp turns, and one-lane bridges. Drive carefully, and don't rush—it's about the journey, not the destination.
- **Guided Tour**: If navigating the tricky roads doesn't appeal to you, a guided tour can be a relaxing and informative option. Tour guides often share interesting stories about the area and know the best stops, including some hidden spots you might not find on your own.

Tips for Beating the Crowds and Staying Safe

The Road to Hana can get busy, so here are some tips to make your trip smoother:

1. **Start Early**: Begin your journey around 6:00 AM to get ahead of the crowds. Early starts also give you more time to explore each stop.
2. **Plan Your Route**: Decide on the must-visit stops ahead of time so you can manage your time wisely.
3. **Drive Slowly**: The road is narrow and has sharp turns, so take it slow and enjoy the views. Yield to oncoming traffic and be patient.
4. **Pack Supplies**: Bring plenty of water, snacks, sunscreen, and a first-aid kit. Cell service is spotty in many areas, so don't rely on GPS.
5. **Respect Nature**: Stay on marked trails and don't pick plants or leave trash behind. Protecting the environment ensures this magical place stays beautiful for generations.

The Unforgettable Journey

The Road to Hana isn't just a drive—it's a full-day adventure that connects you with the heart of Maui. Every stop, from the roaring waterfalls to the peaceful forests, offers a unique experience that will leave you in awe.

By the time the sun began to set, I had reached the end of the road with a heart full of gratitude. The sights, sounds, and moments of this journey were more than just memories; they were stories to share for a lifetime. Whether you drive yourself or take a guided tour, the Road to Hana will show you a side of Maui that is both wild and wonderful.

Hidden Gems of Hawaii: Discovering Off-the-Beaten-Path Wonders

Hawaii is known for its famous beaches, vibrant luaus, and iconic attractions, but there's a quieter, less-explored side of the islands waiting for the curious traveler. These hidden gems offer a chance to connect with the soul of Hawaii—its untouched landscapes, quiet trails, and rich cultural heritage. If you're looking to go beyond the well-trodden paths, these off-the-beaten-path wonders will reveal a Hawaii few get to see.

Molokai's Papohaku Beach: One of Hawaii's Largest White Sand Beaches

Papohaku Beach, located on the serene island of Molokai, is a breathtaking stretch of white sand that feels like a hidden paradise. Spanning nearly three miles, it's one of the largest white sand beaches in Hawaii. Unlike the bustling beaches of Waikiki, Papohaku is often deserted, offering a sense of solitude that's hard to find elsewhere.

Here, the sound of crashing waves replaces the chatter of crowds. It's the perfect place to stroll along the shore, enjoy a peaceful picnic, or simply sit and watch the endless horizon.

Swimming is possible but can be rough depending on the season, so always check local conditions before diving in.

What makes Papohaku special is its untouched beauty. There are no towering hotels or loud beach bars—just you, the sand, and the sea. The nearby town of Maunaloa has a few local shops and eateries where you can grab snacks or talk to locals about the island's history and culture.

Lanai's Garden of the Gods and Shipwreck Beach

Garden of the Gods (Keahiakawelo)
Lanai's Garden of the Gods is a surreal landscape unlike anything else in Hawaii. This rocky, desert-like area is dotted with red and orange boulders that glow under the setting sun, creating an otherworldly scene. According to Hawaiian legend, the area was formed after two kahuna (priests) battled by throwing rocks at each other.

Accessible by a bumpy dirt road, this spot is best visited with a 4WD vehicle. While there are no amenities here, the sense of isolation and the stunning views of Molokai and Maui in the distance make the journey worthwhile.

Shipwreck Beach
Not far from the Garden of the Gods is Shipwreck Beach, a windswept shoreline famous for the ghostly remains of a World War II Liberty Ship stranded on its reef. This beach isn't ideal for swimming due to strong currents, but it's a treasure for history buffs, photographers, and beachcombers. You'll often find shells and driftwood scattered along the shore.

The beach's remote location means you'll likely have it all to yourself, allowing you to soak in the haunting beauty of the shipwreck and the rugged coastline.

The Mysterious Green Sand Beach on Big Island

Tucked away in South Point (Ka Lae), the Green Sand Beach, or Papakōlea, is one of only four green sand beaches in the world. Its unique olive-green color comes from tiny crystals called olivine, formed from volcanic activity.

Getting to the beach is an adventure in itself. You'll need to hike about 2.5 miles along a dusty trail with sweeping views of the ocean. The trek can be challenging under the sun, so bring water, sturdy shoes, and sunscreen. Alternatively, you can hire a local driver with a 4WD vehicle to take you to the beach.

Once you arrive, the sight is unforgettable. The crescent-shaped bay, framed by cliffs, looks like something from a dream. The sand sparkles in the sunlight, and the waters are perfect for a refreshing dip. Because of its remote location, the beach is never crowded, giving you a true sense of escape.

Secret Waterfalls, Lava Tubes & Underrated Hiking Trails

Waterfalls
While Hawaii is known for its iconic waterfalls, some remain hidden from the usual tourist routes. On the Big Island, Kulaniapia Falls is a serene spot tucked away on private property. Visitors can book a stay at the nearby inn or purchase a day pass to access the falls. On Kauai, the Blue Hole hike takes you to the base of Mount Waialeale, where cascading waterfalls form a dramatic amphitheater.

Lava Tubes
Hawaii's volcanic history has created an intricate network of lava tubes, many of which are hidden beneath the islands. The Kaumana Caves on the Big Island offer a chance to explore these natural tunnels. With a flashlight in hand, you can wander through dark, twisting passages formed by ancient lava flows.

Underrated Trails
For hikers looking to escape the crowds, trails like the Polipoli Springs State Park trails on Maui offer a peaceful retreat. Here, you'll find misty forests, stunning views, and a cooler climate that's perfect for hiking. On Oahu, the Pu'u O Mahuka Heiau State Monument combines a short hike with cultural history, offering panoramic views of Waimea Bay.

Immersive Local Cultural Experiences Away from the Crowds

Molokai's Halawa Valley
The Halawa Valley on Molokai is one of the oldest inhabited places in Hawaii. Here, you can join guided tours led by local families who share stories about the valley's history, legends, and cultural practices. You'll also get to see ancient taro patches and learn about traditional Hawaiian farming methods.

Lanai's Cultural Sites
Lanai is home to several lesser-known cultural sites, including ancient petroglyphs and the Kaunolu Village, a former fishing settlement that was once a favorite retreat of King Kamehameha I. Walking through these sites feels like stepping back in time.

Big Island's Merrie Monarch Festival

If you're visiting in the spring, the Merrie Monarch Festival in Hilo is a must-see. This week-long celebration of hula and Hawaiian culture is a more intimate experience than the commercial luaus you'll find elsewhere. From hula competitions to art exhibits, it's a deep dive into the traditions of the islands.

Hawaii's hidden gems aren't just places—they're experiences that bring you closer to the land, the people, and the history of these magical islands. Whether you're exploring a quiet beach, hiking to a secret waterfall, or learning from locals in a remote valley, these moments will stay with you long after your trip ends. So step off the beaten path and discover the Hawaii that few ever get to see.

Final Travel Tips & Making the Most of Your Hawaiian Adventure

Your Hawaiian journey is an unforgettable experience, but thoughtful planning and preparation can make it even more enriching. Whether you're lounging on tropical beaches, hiking rugged volcanic trails, or immersing yourself in the islands' rich culture, these tips will help you maximize your adventure while leaving a positive impact on Hawaii's environment and communities.

Packing Essentials for Different Climates & Activities

Hawaii's diverse microclimates mean you need to pack strategically for various conditions and activities.

Beach and Water Activities

- **Swimwear**: Bring at least two sets of swimwear for beach days, snorkeling, or surfing.
- **Reef-Safe Sunscreen**: Hawaii bans sunscreens with harmful chemicals like oxybenzone and octinoxate to protect its coral reefs. Choose reef-safe options.
- **Water Shoes**: Essential for exploring rocky beaches, tide pools, or lava rock formations.
- **Light Towel and Quick-Dry Clothes**: Perfect for beach hopping or unexpected swims.

Hiking and Outdoor Adventures

- **Comfortable Hiking Shoes**: Trails range from easy walks to rugged treks, so sturdy footwear is a must.
- **Rain Gear**: Some areas, like Hilo or the rainforest trails in Kauai, experience frequent showers. A lightweight waterproof jacket is ideal.
- **Layers**: While the coast is warm, summit areas like Haleakalā on Maui or Mauna Kea on the Big Island can be freezing, so pack a fleece or windbreaker.
- **Daypack**: A small backpack for carrying water, snacks, and essentials during excursions.

Cultural and Urban Exploration

- **Casual Clothes**: Lightweight, breathable fabrics work best for exploring towns and cultural sites.
- **Dressier Attire**: If you plan to attend a luau or dine at upscale restaurants, bring semi-formal outfits.

Miscellaneous Must-Haves

- **Reusable Water Bottle**: Stay hydrated and reduce plastic waste.
- **Bug Spray**: Essential for rainforest hikes or evenings outdoors.
- **Power Bank**: Handy for long days exploring remote areas.
- **Local Guidebook or Apps**: Maps and tips for off-the-beaten-path spots.

Transportation Tips & How to Navigate the Islands

Getting around Hawaii requires some forethought, as each island has its own transportation challenges.

Rental Cars

- **Essential on Most Islands**: Except for Oahu, where public transport is more robust, a rental car is the best way to explore.
- **Book Early**: Demand is high, especially during peak seasons, so reserve your car in advance.
- **Choose the Right Vehicle**: A standard car is fine for most trips, but if you plan to visit remote spots like Lanai's Shipwreck Beach, opt for a 4WD.

Public Transport

- **The Bus on Oahu**: This reliable and affordable system connects major tourist areas, but schedules can be limiting.
- **Island-Specific Shuttles**: Some islands, like Kauai, offer shuttles to popular attractions, but coverage is limited.

Inter-Island Travel

- **Flights**: The quickest way to travel between islands. Hawaiian Airlines and Southwest Airlines are popular options.
- **Ferries**: Available between Maui and Lanai or Molokai, offering scenic and budget-friendly alternatives.

Biking and Walking

- **Biking**: Some areas, like Lahaina in Maui or Kailua on Oahu, are bike-friendly. Rentals are widely available.
- **Walking**: Perfect for exploring towns, beaches, or short trails.

Guided Tours

- Opt for guided tours if you're unfamiliar with driving on narrow or winding roads, such as the Road to Hana. Tours also provide cultural insights from local guides.

Eco-Friendly Travel & Supporting Local Communities

Hawaii's natural beauty is fragile, and the islands face environmental and cultural challenges due to overtourism. Here's how to tread lightly:

Sustainable Practices

- **Leave No Trace**: Pack out all trash, stay on marked trails, and avoid touching wildlife or coral reefs.
- **Conserve Water and Energy**: Be mindful of water usage, especially on islands facing droughts, and turn off lights and AC in accommodations when not needed.

Support Local Businesses

- **Eat Local**: Dine at family-owned restaurants or food trucks offering Hawaiian specialties.
- **Shop Local**: Buy handmade crafts, jewelry, or snacks at farmers' markets to support artisans.
- **Hire Local Guides**: Choose tours led by residents who share their knowledge and preserve traditions.

Be Respectful

- **Cultural Etiquette**: Learn basic Hawaiian words like "aloha" (hello) and "mahalo" (thank you) and respect sacred sites and customs.
- **Avoid Overcrowding**: Visit popular spots early in the morning or during weekdays to reduce strain on the environment.

Avoiding Common Tourist Mistakes

Even the most prepared travelers can fall into these pitfalls:

- **Underestimating the Sun**: Hawaii's sun is intense, even on cloudy days. Apply sunscreen frequently, wear a hat, and stay hydrated.

- **Ignoring Ocean Safety**: Always heed posted signs, check for strong currents, and avoid swimming alone or at unmonitored beaches.
- **Relying Solely on GPS**: Cell service can be spotty in remote areas, so carry a physical map as backup.
- **Overpacking Itineraries**: Hawaii is best enjoyed at a relaxed pace, so leave room for spontaneity.
- **Not Reserving in Advance**: Popular activities like snorkeling at Molokini Crater or visiting Pearl Harbor require advance booking.

Reflecting on Your Hawaiian Experience

As your Hawaiian adventure comes to an end, take time to reflect on the memories you've created. Whether it's the thrill of snorkeling with sea turtles, the awe of standing at a volcanic crater, or the warmth of local hospitality, these moments become part of your story.

Leave Hawaii with a deeper understanding of its culture, respect for its environment, and a heart full of aloha. Remember that your experience was shaped by the people and places you encountered, so consider giving back—whether by donating to local conservation efforts or sharing your journey to inspire mindful travel in others.

Hawaii isn't just a destination—it's a feeling that stays with you long after you've left its shores. By traveling thoughtfully and immersing yourself in the islands' wonders, you'll carry the spirit of aloha wherever your adventures take you next.

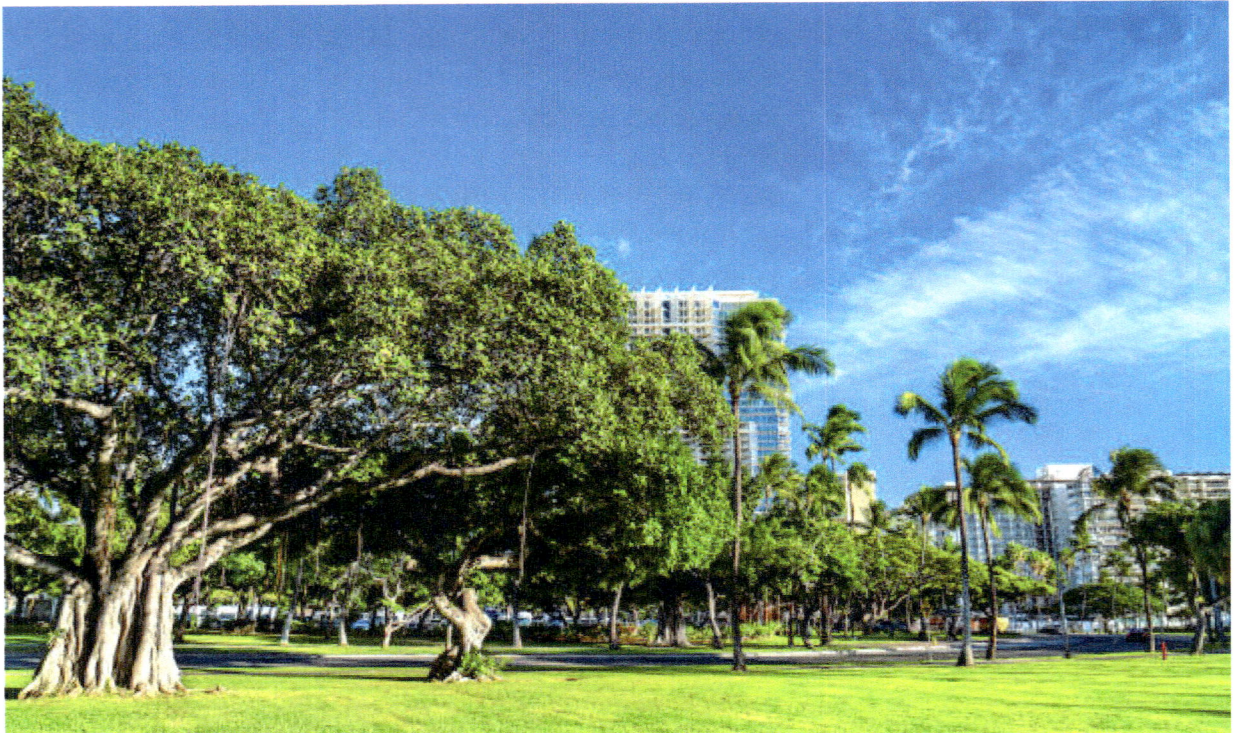

MY EXPERIENCE TO HAWAII

Write about your lovely experience here

_____

_____

_____

_____

_____

_____

_____

_____

_____

_____

_____

_____

Printed in Dunstable, United Kingdom

67209289R00051